Ministry Today

Effectiveness, Fulfillment, and Challenges

Ministry Today

Effectiveness, Fulfillment, and Challenges

by

Helen Doohan

WIPF & STOCK · Eugene, Oregon

Wipf and Stock Publishers
199 W 8th Ave, Suite 3
Eugene, OR 97401

Ministry Today
Effectiveness, Fulfillment, and Challenges
By Doohan, Helen
Copyright©1986 by Doohan, Helen
ISBN 13: 978-1-5326-1563-4

Publication date 4/19/2017
Previously published by Alba House, 1986

To
*Mom and Dad
in appreciation
of your generous
service to the church
and in gratitude and love
for your constant support
of my ministry.*

Acknowledgments

Biblical quotations are from the Revised Standard Version.

Sections of chapter 1 and chapter 5 have appeared in the *Journal of Religion and Health* and *Scripture in Church*. I take this occasion to thank the editors of these journals for the use of material in this book.

Some of the reflections contained in chapter 4 were the result of a series of interviews funded by the Gonzaga Research Council. I wish to thank my colleagues at the university for their support.

Helen Doohan
May 22, 1986

Table Of Contents

INTRODUCTION xiii

CHAPTER 1

Ministry into the 21st century: Issues and Concerns 3

    The Crisis in the Church 3
    Areas of Stress in Ministry 5
    Major Areas of Stress on a Personal Level 7
    Symptoms 9

CHAPTER 2

Burnout: A Personal Phenomenon With Social Repercussions 11

    What Is Burnout? 11
    Burnout as It Relates to Personal Fulfillment 13
    Approaches to the Problem on the
            Individual Level 16
    Burnout as It Relates to Effectiveness
            in Ministry 18
    Stress Factors in Work that Is Ministry 21
    Approaches to the Prevention of Burnout 23

CHAPTER 3

Developing A Spirituality For Ministries 27

    Towards an Understanding of Spirituality 27
    Spirituality's Expression in Ministry 31
        New Testament Perspectives on Ministry 33
        The Ecclesial Dimension of Ministry 37
    Varieties of Ministry within the One Spirituality ... 39
        Spirituality of Ministry as a Response
          to Need 40
    A Spirituality of Wholistic Integration 43

CHAPTER 4

Enhancing Our Approaches To Ministry 49

    Acceptance of the Impact of Stress 50
    The Quality of Work 52
    Approaches and Aids for Growth in Ministry 54
    Support Systems 57
        Profession Support Groups 57
        The Place of Institutions as a Support for
          Ministry 58

CHAPTER 5

Jesus: A Model For All Ecclesial Ministers 61

    The Call to Ministry 62
    The Ministry of Jesus 64
    Response to the Ministry of Jesus 69
    The Ministry of the Disciples 70
    Jesus' Ministry and Ours Today 73

CHAPTER 6

Paul: Effective Ministry As A Leader In The Early Church 77

    Early Leadership in Paul: 1 Thessalonians 79
    Dealing with Crisis: Galatians 82
    Dealing with Diversity: 1-2 Corinthians 87
    A Mature Leadership: Romans 92
    Preparing for an Uncertain Future: Philippians ... 96
    Paul's Leadership in Ministry 99
    Paul and the Professional Christian Minister 100

CHAPTER 7

The Role Of The Leader In Promoting Fulfillment And Effectiveness In Ministry 103

    The Role of the Christian Leader 104
    Promoting Personal Fulfillment and Effectiveness
        in Ministry 106

ENDNOTES 113

BIBLIOGRAPHY 119

INDEX 125

Introduction

Because of the importance of ministry and the key role of the Christian minister in the life of the believing community, I intend to address in this book the issues of personal fulfillment and effectiveness in ministry. My perspective includes, as it must, many issues and concerns, including those problems that often result in varying degrees of stress, burnout and crises, which affect the individual and the community. However, I am most keenly interested in a viable spirituality for the Christian minister, a spirituality that will not only address and prevent the various problems and potential difficulties, but more importantly, lead to the personal growth and fulfillment of the individual. As a Christian people, scripture is a source of our faith and a challenge to our lifestyle. As I read and study the scriptures, I see in Jesus and in Paul powerful models for ministry in the church, many concrete indications of how to deal with crisis and transition, and a continual challenge for personal growth and commitment.

It is my hope that this book will identify the most serious issues involved in ministry in the churches and offer some directions for a more realistic approach to Christian commitment.

Ministry Today

Effectiveness, Fulfillment, and Challenges

Chapter 1

Ministry into the 21st century: Issues and Concerns

We live in critical and crucial times. The arms race, world hunger, oppressive regimes, unscrupulous business practices, and economic injustices are a few of the major problems of our world. These problems unquestionably affect all thinking people and are a particular concern and challenge for committed Christians. These overwhelming issues elicit feelings either of helplessness or recommitment to spheres of personal service. How we deal with the little things in life which confront us on a daily basis often indicates how we will handle the larger issues which likewise challenge us.

Our examination of the issues and concerns facing us in ministry in the last decades of our century includes a perspective on the crisis in the church as well as particular problems and areas of stress in ministry.

The Crisis In The Church

Since the Second Vatican Council, there has been much creative development and many reasons for hope in the Christian community. Renewal has taken on new meaning personally and within parishes and dioceses. The social mission of the church is a part of the consciousness of the vast majority of Christians. The liturgical developments, an emphasis on the church as community, the call to all the baptized to exercise their rights and responsibilities in the world and the church, are a few further examples of positive developments.

The Church finds itself as it approaches the third millennium at a crucial point in history. Part of discerning what direction it must take in the future includes a recognition of some critical factors, among them that of leadership. Not only is there a crisis of leadership in the church today but leaders are subject to criticism and confrontation as never before. A number of present-day leaders continue to utilize primitive leadership styles and to operate out of an inappropriate ecclesiology.[1] The pluralism which characterizes our church is a pluralism regarding theology and praxis. The emergence of laity and women, who recognize their contributions and responsibilities, is notably changing the landscape of life and ministry. Likewise, the unencouraging statistics regarding the decreasing numbers of priests and religious are a concern for all dedicated Christians, the reevaluation of the role of the hierarchy and an examination of structures, alongside a growing emphasis on small groups, are other notable features of the radical changes before us.

The move towards collaborative and intervocational ministries in light of the above issues is also critical. Not only can the Christian community anticipate a redefinition of roles and ministry on the part of religious and priests, but fear, passivity and paralysis can result because of the high expectations placed on these ministers. Education on the part of the laity and lack of education in areas of theology on the part of many priests and religious are other factors to consider.

One encouraging dimension of the crisis is the quest for significant involvement in ministry and for a significant spirituality on the part of priests, religious and laity. In part, this means ability to assume direction for one's personal and group life, to identify one's unique contribution to the larger community, and to move from competition and self-preservation to collaboration and dialogue.

The crisis in the church today is an opportunity for creative development and new strategies. It is a time for discernment, dialogue and cautious optimism. It bears with it our challenge for the future.

Areas Of Stress In Ministry

The ministry of any individual or of groups should be viewed in terms of the needs of the world and the mission of the church. Likewise the tone of the church and the world affect the minister as a person and ultimately the effectiveness of his or her ministry. Life itself has become increasingly more complex causing heightened stress in daily living and in our ability to minister effectively to and with others.

Individuals handle the complexities of life differently depending on their outlook, their priorities and even their health. Some committed people find it very difficult to separate their devotion to their work from their personal choices and their own lifestyle. This attitude manifests itself in giving to the point of strain or exhaustion, or in the inability to say "no." These people never take sufficient time away from their particular ministry and get so caught up in activity that there is little interest in or ability to do anything else. Often they have no set hours for work and vague or non-existent job descriptions.

Church personnel, in their zeal and enthusiasm, often set goals beyond what any single person could accomplish in a given day, month or year. Likewise, they often find it difficult to accept limitations and to share or delegate responsibility. The problem is augmented when a person likes his or her work and has initial enthusiasm for the job or project. However people who set unrealistic goals rarely receive the affirmation or support they need, creating for themselves another situation of stress. Rather than using the normal outlets to relieve the tension, some persons resort to further self-sacrifice and prayer to overcome the obstacles they themselves have created.

Others who see work as a barometer of dedication, seem to cling to their burdens. Guilt, feelings of wasting time when not working, being solely responsible, and the "savior" mentality contribute to the cycle of the problem. A rigidity of behavior leads to isolation as well as long term ineffectiveness. At times, institutional commitments on the part of religious orders and dioceses, militate against a more creative approach to ministry and an assessment of the personal strengths of the individual involved in ministry. The minister begins to experience a lack of support, a feeling of loneliness, a lack of affirmation in areas that count. Former interests begin to fade, fatigue becomes a problem and the individual is less able to cope with demands. Others notice a lack of fresh ideas. Ironically, the last person to note the cycle of distress and realize what is happening is the one experiencing the stress or possibly the burnout.

Stress itself is to be expected in the times in which we live. In terms of religious persons with a commitment to the church, the ecclesiastical changes themselves are stressful and frequently intimidating. There has been little education for transition, change and crisis management. Because of changing roles, some priests and religious feel threatened, while laity whose ministry is also a job, have great pressures to maintain their effectiveness and enhance their value to an organization.

Even without these somewhat negative aspects, the necessity for creative development and new approaches to ministry is stressful. Some people can work or live under pressure, while others easily become distressed or incapacitated. For certain individuals, especially those who expect perfection of themselves and others, the down escalator soon reaches bottom. Only then is the minister forced to assess himself or herself realistically and to begin to accept the ministry of others on their behalf.

Another dimension of stress in ministry is a financial one. This area is generally assumed to be of concern to the laity because of personal and family responsibilities. However, religious often work for less pay at a time when their salaries are essential contributions to a graying community. In addition, some religious and priests commit themselves to higher paying administrative jobs for which they have little attraction or preparation for the sake of providing a good salary to the community. For many reasons, poverty, detachment, obedience, simplicity of lifestyle and commitment to ministry seem to need reassessment.

Major Areas Of Stress On A Personal Level

Among the many potential areas of stress, dedicated people frequently mention the following: perfectionist tendencies, lack of a sense of self-worth, limitations of time and energy to meet the demands of the job, resistance to change on the part of others, inability to work with a group, inability to accept another's point of view, independence, anger at situations in the church, fatigue, inability to relax, inability to achieve balance between work and personal needs, lack of recognition or affirmation, too little work, community life, unwanted leadership roles, etc.

Some of the above are self-induced or self-perpetuated, while several are situational or depend on others' responses or reactions. In certain instances the person can alleviate the situation of personal stress by removing the causes. In other circumstances, where the individual is unable to remove the cause of the stress, he or she can at least change his or her attitude toward the stressful situation.

At times, environmental factors such as noise, traffic, telephone interruptions are identified as sources of stress. Living with people with different value systems or with those who lack self-discipline is also stressful. Perhaps there is a larger problem that is the real issue in some of these instances and the minister will need to surface his or her unconscious motivations and attitudes.

Finally, ministry in the church is itself a source of real stress. How difficult it is to have to always deal with the criticism of administration or the hesitancy of church leadership to delegate. Constant opposition to new ideas and judgmental attitudes are also a problem especially in a period of transition. Deadlines and an aura of immediacy can be devastating. Religious women who feel they know what their role is comment on the stress they feel in being pressured to return to a past they have previously been asked to leave. Many persons in ministry must deal with disturbed or difficult people and have an inability to distance themselves from these pressures. Lack of self-confidence or training are also hard on one and inhibit personal fulfillment and effectiveness in ministry.

Symptoms Of Stress

Rather than being an elusive phenomenon, the effects of an overly stressful life are quite tangible. This stress is manifested in physical signs and symptoms associated with illness. Among these are headache, insomnia, loss of appetite, irritability, tiredness, chest pain, lack of energy and depression. Stress is also an underlying factor when typically committed people complain of lack of energy or desire to go to the place of work, are unable to associate with companions, place the blame on others, exhibit a lack of caring for anything, are constantly discouraged or angry at the expectations of others, question their own worth, are supersensitive to casual remarks, unable to concentrate or pray and lack peace.

In the last ten years, much has been written on the kind of stress that leads to burnout and the stress associated with mid-life transitions. Many dedicated priests, religious and laity have experienced feelings of the kind of hopelessness and loss of enthusiasm that is so often described in terms and categories consistent with the stress-burnout syndrome.[2] It is, therefore, appropriate I think to turn our attention to this issue in order to assess what has become one of the major concerns in present-day ministry. An analysis of the literature, a synthesis of the problem and an overview of possible directions may give us a solid foundation from which to proceed.

CHAPTER 2

BURNOUT[1]:
A Personal Phenomenon With Social Repercussions

Recent literature reveals a copious amount of material on the phenomenon of burnout and its prelude, stress. No one is immune. Burnout — a depression-related syndrome — is observed in teachers, administrators, child-care workers, nurses, leaders, clergy and religious. While stress can be a positive aspect of the human condition in so far as it can generate creative responses, the emphasis is shifting to the negative dimensions of stress that lead to burnout. Coping, adaptation and survival constitute the language of the articles. Some of the questions we will be addressing here are: What is burnout? Why is it a critical issue today? How can persons creatively approach the stress of contemporary life?

What Is Burnout?

Burnout is described by Kramer as "a physical, emotional, psychological and spiritual phenomenon — an experience of personal fatigue, alienation, failure and more."[2] It involves a ". . . progressive loss of idealism, energy and purpose experienced by people in the helping professions."[3] Persons are exhausted physically and emotionally. Distancing from others, regarding efforts as failure and abandoning work are the extreme manifestations of the disillusionment and frustration associated with burnout.[4] It is the exact opposite of feeling fulfilled in one's life and ministry.

The burnout syndrome with its physical and emotional exhaustion results from stress.[5] While stress can be ordinary or extraordinary, the stress factor in burnout is a pressure that ". . . exceeds the ability of the individual to cope. . . Stress becomes 'distress' and may result in physical symptoms, feelings of inadequacy or being overwhelmed, a crisis of faith and/or difficulty with or inability to pray."[6] Stress arises from a variety of quarters — interpersonal clashes, excessively taxing administrative responsibilities, time constraints and conflicting role expectations.[7] In this regard, burnout is seen as a "special form of stress reaction to work and to organizational pressures. It occurs in people who are motivated by idealistic values of service and professional goals, in addition to the usual reasons for work."[8]

The stages of burnout are described in several ways. Jones and Emmanuel speak of "heating up," "boiling," and "exploding". In the first stage, dissatisfaction, isolation and lack of appreciation are experienced. Then a feeling of helplessness emerges and a question of usefulness and efficacy. The frustration becomes open rebellion or mechanical performance in the final stage.[9] According to Gill, a person can continue work as usual in the first stage, but job performance begins to suffer somewhat in the second. Only in the third and most severe degree of burnout is there a complete disruption in work.[10] Terminal burnout is described briefly as "when someone becomes sour on one's self, humanity and everybody."[11] Intense feelings of loneliness are characteristic of this stage.

There seems to be a consensus on the causes of burnout. Conflict between needs and accomplishment, unrealistic dedication, use of work as a substitute for a satisfying personal life, an authoritarian management style and an inability to delegate authority and say no to unreasonable demands are causes noted by Clark,[12] Gill,[13] and Swogger.[14] In addition, Gill also identifies a lack of talent or ability to achieve a goal, inadequate education or training, overidentification with those served and an inability to communicate strong feelings.[15]

Burnout As It Relates To Personal Fulfillment

Burnout is a growing problem in contemporary society. Why? What issues are involved?

Among the forces that lead to the development of burnout syndrome, five are particularly significant and critical. The first issue of importance is the *difficulty of diagnosis* and identification of burnout. The indications of potential burnout are similar to those of an impending heart attack. Carlton and Brown, noting the signals of an impending heart attack as enumerated by Mackenzie, refer to indications frequently experienced by burnout candidates: (1) feeling indispensable, (2) finding no time to work on important things, (3) taking on too much, not being able to say no, (4) always feeling the constant unrelenting pressure of being "behind," (5) habitually long work days [12-14 hours], (6) feelings of guilt at leaving work on time, (7) taking office problems home.[16]

The same authors speak about stressful administrative tasks which, when consistent and extreme, also lead to psychiatric and somatic disorders. To complicate matters, the criteria for diagnosing a major depressive episode are strikingly similar to signs and symptoms of burnout. Among the signs of both syndromes are loss of interest, concern and enthusiasm, decreased energy, disturbance of appetite and sleep patterns, mood changes, feelings of worthlessness and guilt, difficulty in concentrating, somatic disorders and uncharacteristic behavior.[17] Finally, many persons consider themselves to be immune and so ignore the warnings.[18] Others are excessively fearful and thus compound the signals. No wonder diagnosis is difficult!

A second issue is the relation between the *existential situation* and the person. A recent study suggests "that it may be as important to understand which characteristic of individuals determine responses to stressful life events as it is to understand qualities of the events themselves."[19] Individuals perceive events differently, and they assign varying degrees of significance to events. In fact, individual differences account for the variety of responses to situations that arouse anxiety.[20] Many experiences are filled with too many stressful components that threaten a person's equilibrium.[21] Stimulus-overload affects everyone, although there are individual levels of coping.

For a select population, other factors are involved. "Most priests know that their own personalities are a source of genuine stress, especially in the confoundings that they regularly experience in understanding their own sexuality."[22] Furthermore, "while the realm of intimacy has been over romanticized it is difficult to deny that systematic exclusion of close relationships, except with males, has as an ideal been a source of continuing stress for priests."[23]

The whole person responds or reacts to stressful situations. Personality and life situation often determine how an individual will cope. Because stress is the stepping stone to burnout, consideration of personal abilities and liabilities is essential.

A third factor affecting burnout is "... the sheer weight of *change* — change in society, in values, in physical environments, in organizations and in our personal selves."[24] Change calls for adaptation and refocusing. Values are often called into question. Plans are upset. In contemporary society adaptation must occur at an accelerated pace. A stressful situation ensues, resistance is lowered and complete disintegration follows.

The *increasing demands of ministry* and the dedication of committed people are a fourth issue to be considered. Freudenberger describes a number of characteristics that are predispositions to burnout in dedicated people. He observes that these people "... experience a great deal of internal and external pressure to succeed, to make work go well and to help more and more people. They face equally extreme measures of distress and guilt if the ideal is not achieved."[25]

Religious people who work with distressed, deprived or demanding people, who are responsible for too many and who are perfectionists or too idealistic are likely candidates for burnout.[26] For persons familiar with religious formation, the above categories and others mentioned by Gill were frequently fostered in an earlier style of novitiate training. A large segment of the church has been unrealistically trained and now needs retraining. In addition, the contemporary demands of ministry are frequently outside the academic preparation of ministers. When a committed person perceives himself or herself as inadequate, stress and guilt develop. This combination is a precondition for burnout and is all too prevalent.

Furthermore, "The lack of a healthy, profoundly human model of spiritual development remains a major stress on all ministers today."[27] Because of the lack of role models, overcommitment and/or isolation may prevail. These conditions foster the development of burnout.

Finally, a fifth issue that contributes significantly to the increase in burnout victims is the *narrow perception of leisure.* Leisure as a social problem emerged after World War II. Part of the problem is the understanding of leisure as a euphemism for idleness, laziness and non-productivity.[28] While there is a relationship between leisure, free time and relaxation, confusion exists as to the nature of the relationship.[29] Opposite extremes are evident in people doing nothing or filling time with everything available for consumption. Frequently the structures in church and society militate against a creative use of leisure.[30] The need for an intelligent understanding and use of leisure is obvious. Because its absence contributes to the problem of stress and burnout, creative solutions are considered a necessity.

Approaches To The Problem On The Individual Level

Among the many viable approaches to the problem of burnout, several are considered essential. These are prevention, self-assessment, adaptation to change, reevaluation of ministry and creative leisure.

Prevention of burnout includes proper nutrition, regular exercise, time for play, laughter, relaxation and reflection.[31] The acquisition of self-knowledge, the comments of supportive friends, the development of professional knowledge, will keep stress within acceptable limits.[32] In addition, focusing on reality, clarifying roles, involving others, setting priorities and evaluating the situation all contribute to burnout prevention. While many factors are involved, prevention is the best medicine.

Each individual has an optimum stress level. *Self-assessment* includes knowledge of the right amount and kind of stress, of the appropriate time frames and of the types of circumstances that are likely to result in acceptable levels of stress.[33] Balance in life is important for coping. Talking with peers, positive reinforcement and examination of alternatives can help one deal with the various stages of burnout.[34] Recovery is possible, but it demands honesty and acceptance of personal responsibility. Guidance and counseling must be available for the extreme case. Perhaps stress counseling will be a specialization of the future.

Also needed is a *new approach to change*. Persons must prepare themselves for the future. Planning, direction and responsibility are the order of the day. Persons and groups need an ability to adapt. "Fortunately most of us have the capacity to adapt to the vagaries and the exigencies of life's stressors without suffering the chronic and often debilitating effects of distress."[35] Anticipation and preparation are the coping techniques to be developed. Many of the prospective planning methods offer insight into this process.

A *reevaluation of ministry* can also prove to be an effective approach to burnout. Ministers must discern, understand and confront the question of stress in ministry. Peer support and dialogue groups would facilitate this assessment. In addition, "Spirituality can deal with stress which arises because of a failure to integrate what one does in ministry with who one is as a person called to be a minister of the Gospel."[36] The integration of ministry and life will foster the growth of authentic models for committed people. However, there must be a recognition of human needs and responses so that a model of health and wholeness will emerge. "What is needed is a change of values that can come about only by a change in our interior vision."[37]

Perhaps the most inclusive approach to the problem of burnout is the *creative development of leisure*. The integration called for in ministry and the vision needed to live fully are attainable only when leisure permeates life. Leisure is more than faith.[38] "Genuine leisure culminates in the religious."[39] If leisure is the contemplation and the celebration of life, as Aristotle perceived it, then the leisure experience will be a joyful and restorative antidote to burnout.[40] In fact, leisure, rightly approached, can be the preventive measure for the malady of dedicated people.

Burnout As It Relates To Effectiveness In Ministry

Perhaps the most insightful aspects of the phenomenon of burnout for our purposes occur in the literature that emphasizes expectations, especially as it relates to ministry. For many, burnout means a disparity between expectations and achievement.[41] There is a nagging sense of incompleteness and a lack of fulfillment in many dedicated persons. In these instances, burnout can result from high expectations and over-challenge in the ministry or low expectations and under-challenge.[42] These expectations can be either personal aspirations or suggested by others. Burnout is, therefore, the result of internal as well as external factors. The situation itself can cause burnout if the individual is unable to respond appropriately. Conversely, a person can be well on the road to burnout even though a given situation is objectively neutral or even positive. In this instance, the difficulty lies primarily with the individual.

A prolific writer on the topic of burnout strongly suggests that burnout is a function of a bad situation in which idealistic people must continually operate. The bad situation destroys human values rather than promotes them.

Therefore, burnout results from a negative situation or environment, not from bad people who are cold and uncaring.[43] This observation offers some food for thought regarding burnout in ministry.[44] It also challenges us to look at the job in terms of the broader societal situation as well as in terms of the person.

There is a close relationship between cultural paradigms or models and personal identity.[45] Indeed, "The roots of burnout, of personal identity, are very much implanted in the paradigm of the modern temporary world."[46] Our society is continually setting new goals and changing. There is also an emphasis on youthfulness and wealth. Roles are seen as transitory in a very temporary world. Uncertainty results because of the rapidity of change that is required. Traditions are often reduced to ashes. The traditional support networks that sustain and reinforce persons are being snuffed out.[47] Family ties and community involvement are on the wane and with them the traditional supportive components of human existence. If people feel trapped and unable to control events, and if people also lack genuine support systems, then burnout is the expected outcome. Our society seems to be contributing to this end result.

However, another aspect also warrants our consideration. Some individuals begin to look to the job for the emotional supports that are lacking in other areas of life. If these expectations are unreal or unmet, then frustration and dissatisfaction can occur and one loses his or her effectiveness as a minister.

In addition to the movements in society, certain job design factors carry with them a high potential for burnout. These include: monotonous or meaningless work, little human interaction, devaluation of work over the last two to three years, and devaluation of the profession itself.

Conversely a positive atmosphere, appropriate feedback, opportunity for development and high prestige, constitute a low potential for burnout.[48] If a person is under stress, then decision-making skills, job interest and technical performance are usually affected. Furthermore, role-conflict as a source of stress also affects performance and job retention. Likewise, when the organization itself is under stress, the managers or workers experience it as well.[49] The system, therefore, can generate undue stress and in doing so, contribute to burnout. These factors which affect work life are no respecters of persons. These significant factors influence priests, religious and laity in ministry as well as their counterparts in society.

On another level, attitudes regarding work hinder or enhance performance. The work ethic has not disappeared. People are still willing to work hard, providing they can influence the nature of their jobs and pursue their own lifestyle.[50] However, persons who are fulfilled in and through their work also have an ability to wholeheartedly choose their work.[51] They "want to do" what others "have to do." The issue is not one of being overinvolved or working too little. Rather, it is the attitude persons bring to work which determine this creative utilization of stress or their succumbing to distress. Attitudes toward work and toward life affect a person's resiliency to respond appropriately to unique situations. They can also lead to the problem of work-fixation which is attributed to the combination of competency, unfulfilled needs and overwork.[52]

Society contributes to stress and job factors contribute to stress. We have observed that the environment can and often does contribute to the stress that leads to burnout. The individual, in some ways, is a victim of these circumstances. However, only certain individuals perceive these stresses as distressing. Why?

One author comments, "The problem is not so much the environment as it is one's interpretation of it."[53] Personal development, self-awareness and reality orientation are necessary components that assure the quality of our life and the quality of our ministry. Expectations and reality seem to differ for many people. Frustration causes symptoms that increasingly need professional attention. Although coping skills differ among individuals, a significant number of persons are adversely affected by the stress of life and are unable to cope effectively. Indeed, the medical community devotes one half to three quarters of its routine medical practice to stress related complaints.[54] Society, the job and the person contribute to the problem, and perhaps also to the solution.

Stress Factors In Work That Is Ministry

While the insights on burnout in the general literature can readily be applied to persons in ministry, some additional factors are worth considering here. If the typical burnout candidate is described as charismatic, energetic, impatient, given to high standards, giving all in whatever is done and expecting rewards commensurate with effort, then these characteristics are intensified in the person called to ministry in the priesthood, religious life and lay professional services. In the period prior to and immediately following the Second Vatican Council, the priesthood and religious life attracted very idealistic and generous persons in the Catholic community. The qualities in these candidates would serve them well in a stable but growing church.

However, the person in ministry today, serves in a church in transition and in a church in crisis. A better informed laity and society are more critical and questioning of authority and of traditional roles. Views of church are changing and expanding. Some segments of the church are responding with strict and rigid rules while others are exploring new ways of living out their Christian commitment. The professional minister is often caught in the middle between institutions, structures and traditions on the one hand, and a pluralism of ideas and approaches on the other. The situation of the church is affecting those in ministry and impinges on their effectiveness as well.

Role-conflict and differing expectations also touch those in ministry. Not only do colleagues differ regarding their understanding of the essence of the church, priesthood and religious life, but the laity are increasingly vocal in what they expect from themselves and religious personnel. If the person in ministry does not have a strong sense of self-identity and self-direction, then the conflict is intensified because of the diverse options and opinions. This situation was not the case during the formative period of most clergy and religious.

The nature of the work also intensifies predispositions to burnout in priests, religious and laity. Characteristically, religious personnel serve the needy. Persons in need are often demanding as well as ungrateful, draining the minister to a precarious point. Since professional ministers have usually been trained to work tirelessly, there is often little room for total personal development. A very narrow view of life can result with too much emphasis placed on the work of ministry.

Furthermore, the implications of faith as a motivator give extra energy to the minister but can also lead to serious forms of denial. There is a tendency to place oneself in the hands of God prematurely when difficulties are encountered. In a period of transition and change, mistakes will be made and time will be needed for assessment and redirection. Can the religious give themselves the permission to be less than "perfect" in a period of transition? Some early formative training militates against this approach.

Likewise, priests and religious will need to be more aware that the progression from the honeymoon stage to crisis and apathy in ministry can apply to themselves as well as to others.[55] No one is immune. As options increase for dedicated Christian persons, so does the potential for burnout. Religious today have more options on the level of life and ministry and probably less training to deal with them. This, too, has an influence on their effectiveness.

Finally, because of idealism, dedication and commitment, those professional ministers who are underchallenged within church situations can experience increased frustration. Creative and dedicated people deserve an outlet for their energy in service and in development. Structures that are no longer life-giving must be reassessed. Routine or dead-end situations are particularly difficult for the kind of person attracted to the specialized ministries in the church. These factors add to the potential for burnout. And with burnout comes the serious problem of personnel retention.

Approaches To The Prevention Of Burnout

While burnout is a concern for all persons involved in the service professions, burnout among professional ministers is a special concern in the community of faith. As numbers decrease, the demands and pressures on those persons remaining in these groups will increase. What approaches are advocated for the prevention of burnout? Will these approaches retain the existing personnel and make their lifestyle appealing to a new generation of potential priests and religious? Or is the church facing a radically new experience in terms of ministry and commitment? These questions are urgent and many groups are just now beginning to address them.

A first step in dealing with the problem of stress in ministry is to *admit the seriousness of stress* in the life of the religious minister.[56] In addition, the Bishops' Committee emphasizes a needed balance in priestly life with attention given to *prayer, work, friendship and leisure.*[57] Furthermore, *theological approaches* and a viable understanding of church are integral to the solution of stress related problems. We are dealing with dedicated persons who are experiencing stress because of religious, personal and societal factors. It is suggested that the approaches deal with all of these areas.

Education and re-education seem to be essential. A deep sense of vocation and of commitment bring with it renewed energy and vitality.[58] Developing this *vocational sense* is important. A realization of call and a depth of response is facilitated in reflective or contemplative moments. These moments are closely related to leisure, time, space and presence. Therefore, a new *expansive attitude towards life* is essential. In this approach, a new identity is formed within the minister, a sense of identity that can grow and evolve with time.[59] It is an identity that emerges from the foundations of a person's very being and not from the work at hand.

In the process of educating for a new orientation to life, some concrete approaches can be implemented. For example, *human resource planning*, which is developing in church administration, should be encouraged.[60] This is a very important area in pastoral planning because it deals with people before programs. In addition, the evaluation and the assessment of ministers is an integral feature. *Support* and *encouragement* are a part of the evaluative process. *Feedback* by a significant person can be affirming and stimulating. This approach can also provide an opening for crisis prevention and crisis intervention.[61] Within the context of human resource planning, church policies are periodically reviewed and the mission of the church reevaluated. Perhaps obligatory celibacy and liturgical practices will be identified as needing revision. Committed religious and priests involved in church life are increasingly finding it necessary to identify stress and growth experiences and to plan realistically for the church of the future. Readjustments in ritual and regulation seem only a matter of time.

Church personnel are also encouraged to learn from other organizations and groups. Organizations are *redefining* the essence of *success* in that success does not necessarily mean promotion.[62] Descriptive feedback rather than criticism is utilized on the job.[63] Innovative approaches to work, loose supervision, quality of work life and job variety are considered in the market place.[64] These areas are readily applicable to church life and can foster a more satisfying ministry for church personnel. Furthermore, formal preparations for ministry, as for careers, can be designed to include training for the reduction of stress and tedium.[65]

Another approach is the *fostering of personal responsibility* and *personal development* among professional ministers. The individual has the power to change his or her perception of a difficult situation. The individual can also identify the true source of stress and respond accordingly. He or she can begin to set realistic goals personally and in terms of ministry. It is said that "if expectations are more carefully developed and more under the control of the individual, burnout is less likely. Therefore, the solution for burnout is not in the environment but within the individual. The ultimate is a change in the self-concept."[66]

A *healthy* sense of personal identity and *self-esteem* is essential in order to deal realistically with the expectations of others.[67] Furthermore, professional ministers should be encouraged to relax and to enjoy their accomplishments before moving on to new experiences.[68] This dimension seems especially important in a period of questioning, crisis and criticism. The person in ministry today needs a self-anchoring rather than a role-identity. Time spent in this area will insure resiliency and the ability to adapt to new situations.

Support systems should be encouraged. People involved in the same work in different settings can give useful advice and provide technical and emotional support.[69] The feeling of being loved, being valued and cared for often results from these supportive networks. *Social contacts* bolster personal identity and are a significant feature in job satisfaction.[70] The best predictor of longevity in a job or in ministry is *job satisfaction!*[71]

Persons in ministry have new options open to them as they serve a renewed church and a very different world. However, they can be reeducated for today and for the future. They can learn to deal more effectively with stress, the prelude to burnout, and can reformulate their goals and expectations.[72] Assistance in these areas must be available if the existing personnel are to find fulfillment in their lives and become more effective in their ministry. Future candidates will be attracted to priestly and religious life as well as to the lay ministry as new models emerge and as ministry by these groups is perceived as personally satisfying, hopeful and liberating.

The focus on the professional minister in this chapter — and especially on the religious and priest — was intentional since these ministers are visible models in their commitment for all Christians. Their successes and failures can offer direction for the development of a viable spirituality for the many dedicated persons who minister in the church. This is the area we will be covering in chapter 3.

CHAPTER 3

Developing A Spirituality For Ministers

In order to be effective in ministry, it is advisable for the Christian minister not only to identify the areas of stress in his or her life, such as we spoke about in the first two chapters, but also to develop an integrated and satisfying approach to life as a whole. This lived experience of the Christian life or spirituality reflects the individuality of the person in ministry, the traditions of the church and the world, and the culture of a particular time and place. In this chapter we will approach the topic of a spirituality for ministers by identifying the components of spirituality, exploring the expressions of a spirituality within the context of ministry, and highlighting the aspects that lead to a sense of personal fulfillment and effectiveness in ministry.

Towards An Understanding Of Spirituality

A spirituality for the person involved in Christian ministry can be described in terms of its unity of purpose or unifying focus. This unity of life is based primarily on one's relationship with the Lord, a relationship cultivated in prayer, in sharing in faith, in study of the gospels and in a contemplative insight into life experiences. From this unity, or centering, of life, the religious, priest or lay person will increasingly develop an ability to be involved in the multiplicity of activities associated with ministry with a unity of purpose.[1] Concentrating on the meaning of our existence, on our motivation, on the meaning of experience, enables us to make sense out of our individual and communal world. The result of this process is that ministry becomes "action out of meaning" and a vital expression of our faith in God's presence in history.[2]

Spirituality and its expression in ministry are intimately connected. There is a flow of energy between the two, or more correctly, one expresses and defines the other. However, spirituality tends to be an elusive phenomenon unless the various components are identified and related to the existential experience. It is to these constitutive components that we now turn.

If the heart of Christian spirituality is a person's relationship with the Lord, then a significant means of divine encounter is *prayer*. The Christian strives to always be in readiness to experience the presence of God. However prayer is only a small part of what Ernest Larkin identifies as the *contemplative way*.[3]

There are three aspects of the contemplative way, first, *self-knowledge* which presumes solitude and humility; second, *centering* prayer which leads to contemplation which is God breaking into our consciousness and experienced in love and union; third, *relationships* encountered in friendships, community and ministry. These aspects of the contemplative journey have the central component of *receptivity* as their characteristic quality. This quality is frequently missing in the active minister yet is essential if the unifying force is to be discovered.

Self-knowledge attained in contemplation leads to the identification of one's false self, a self in need of reconciliation, mortification and humility. Human weakness, the reality of personal and social sin, are known and acknowledged. There is a desire to experience our full personalities so that there can be a movement towards integration. Loneliness is perceived as a fact of life; anger is seen as a response to the inner dichotomies and external pressures that still exist. However, as the initial step of self-knowledge increases the person develops self-esteem and experiences the freedom that encourages self-gift.

The contemplative or prayer movement is an expression of *faith*, the expression becoming more spontaneous and more authentic as the person matures as a Christian. Here faith is not a denial of life[4] but a placing of ourselves in the presence of the Lord so that fear can be overcome and freedom embraced. It is an adult faith that asserts itself in challenge before the Lord. It forms us in a spirituality that can integrate who we are and what we do as servants of the gospel. This component of spirituality focuses on the strength emerging from the center, from deep within the person. It is discovered in the kind of leisure that culminates in the religious expressions of life, and is celebrated liturgically.[5]

The relational dimensions of the contemplative way are the expressions and the sources of the life force within us. Friendship is mutual, community is life-giving, ministry is effective. We are loving signs of what it means to be church. In our relationships we witness to gospel values in a temporary and transitory world. The contemporary cultural emphasis on youth, wealth, and power is replaced by the Christian acceptance of the individual, poverty and weakness. Thus, the interior quality of spirituality is expressed apostolically in the contemplative way.[6]

There are other components in a significant spirituality for the ministering person and qualities expressive of it. The use and development of the *imagination* is a critical component of contemporary spirituality. Imagination, unlike fantasy, builds on facts, truth and reality.[7] It is a creative and hopeful power within each of us. It taps the intuitive rather than the reasoned dimensions of our being. The intuition is the "felt" meaning that motivates us, the stuff of dreams, the sudden breakthrough or insight.[8] Imagination is appreciated for its breadth and depth; thinking is but a pale reflection of it. The use of the imagination and intuition can enhance the vision necessary for ministry today. These aspects of the human person surface in the integrating, prayerful moments of life.

The development of any spirituality needs maturing, direction, awareness of biblical roots and ecclesial traditions, silence, dialogue, theological reflection and asceticism. It then becomes a spirituality capable of identifying the gaps in our world, that sees the aspects of technology that work against us. It suggests alternatives to the negative aspects of our environment. For example, because of technology we can have a world in which there is always light and day. We never have to deal with the night. A contemporary spirituality asks how can we embrace the darkness with its intimacy, quiet and unconscious strength in the context of our modern world. Can we negotiate and collaborate with others, be sensual rather than compete with our rational strengths alone? A spirituality of the ministering person identifies these alternate emphases as significant. But in order to appreciate these realities, the minister cannot afford to be distracted constantly by a hectic life style. Rather, the Christian involved in ministry is called to a level of *integration* in his or her life so that he or she can continually draw upon an unusual reserve of energy. This means that work and leisure are approached with the same sense of call and attitude of love.

The unity we spoke of earlier becomes a lived reality. It is a point in our existence when we understand the quality of integrity. Integrity means that we face ourselves and accept ourselves. It acknowledges and confesses oneself a sinner, while believing that God has more in mind for each of us. Integrity brings brokenness and wholeness together and allows God to work within us so that we can grow as a child of God.[9]

Spirituality for the Christian is the process of growth in our personhood, lived out in terms of our relationship to ourselves, God and others. It is the fabric of our lives which gives us the strength and the focus to truly serve others as the gospel demands. In fact, our spirituality is rightly expressed in service in the church and in the world in which we live.

Spirituality's Expression In Ministry

While much more can be said about spirituality, I would like to turn our attention to a particular aspect of Christian life, our outreach in ministry. Ministry is described in different ways from New Testament times to the present day. Christian ministry is lived out in the community of faith and consists of identifiable component parts. Furthermore, *ministry is a response to needs*, needs in the ministering person and in the recipients of the service. Ministry in the future will be different and, to the degree that it is, we will find it necessary to prepare ourselves for that future. These are the dimensions of ministry that I will examine in order to understand more fully this lived expression of our spirituality.

Theological reflection and assessment of ministry is in a

state of transition and growth. There is a restrictive understanding which emphasizes ministry as a designation of certain "positions of leadership and service within the Christian community," as opposed to ministry being synonymous with the "priesthood of the laity," with "reponsible discipleship," or "with living out one's baptismal commitment."[10] We recognize that some distinctions, as O'Meara points out, find their foundation in legal decision and not in essential distinctions in church service;[11] and that there is likewise a "professional ministry" characterized by call and extensive preparation, full-time, possibly life-time commitment, which is considered foundational for the church in its life.[12] While these ministries and the ministers within these roles are certainly in the forefront of many minds, we must not neglect to emphasize the other dimensions of ministry, ministry as an aspect of the life of all the baptized.[13] For those within and outside the church, it is ministry by the believing Christian that makes Christ a present and living reality.

Ministry is the reflection of what we believe as Christians. It is the responsibility of all who are called to be disciples and flows from the gifts of the Spirit given to individuals for the benefit of the community. Viewing ministry as discipleship avoids the sharp distinctions between those ministered to and the minister since all are considered learners and followers in the Lord.[14] However, while there is an equality in our call to ministry, ministry itself requires a responsible and consistent decision to be servant and sign. It is not a hobby[15] or a passing interest. It is a part of our identity as Christians; it is an essential expression of the spirituality of all the baptized. For ministers, the reality of ministry should relieve some of the stress involved in the decreased numbers of priests and religious with the ever increasing demands. Many persons are being called in our time, and many are responding with renewed dedication. Christians are becoming fully alive again.

In our period, as in the early church, questions are being raised by the believing community reflecting on its call. There is an emergence of a variety of gifts among diverse people that is changing the face of the church. Laity and women are asking "Why not?" as they begin to anticipate new issues and new needs. The spirituality of all the baptized is being expressed in ministry. A glance at the New Testament will remind us that the broader meaning of ministry which seems to be emerging today was a reality for the early church.

New Testament Perspectives On Ministry

The New Testament gives us a broad base from which to interpret ministry and to reinterpret it in our own day. Because of the plurality of the traditions we have received, there is room for a variety of interpretations of Christian life and praxis. The gospels, Paul, Acts and the later letters each tell their own story for a different community and a different cultural context. These writings convey complementary insights and enrich our perspective of the early church.

In 1 Corinthians 12:4-12, Romans 12:8, and Ephesians 4:11-14, there are a variety of gifts or ministries: preaching with wisdom, instruction, faith, miracles, healing, prophecy, discernment, speaking in and interpreting tongues. There are the ministries of administration, teaching, almsgiving and hospitality, as well as those of the apostles, evangelists, pastors, prophets and teachers who unify the work of service for the building up of the body of Christ. There is a broad understanding of ministry implied in many of the biblical texts (Ep 4:4-14; Col 1:9-23; 2 Cor 5:14-15; Gal 6:10; Ph 2:8), as well as an emphasis on the origin of the gifts in the Spirit and the centrality of Christ for the Christian minister (Ph 3:7-8). In the gospel conclusions, Christ sends his followers to be ministers of the good news to the ends of the earth and promises to be with them always.

The texts confirm that the entire community of believers shares activity in ministry. This ministry includes the preaching of the gospel and witnessing to the death and resurrection of Jesus, as well as the usual kinds of service rendered to alleviate obvious human need. These charisms, ministering charisms, nourish and expand the church. They are linked to the building up of the body of Christ. Indeed, "every ministry is grounded in charism; some charisms in each Christian lead to ministry."[16]

It is interesting to observe how the New Testament urges and invites ministry, describes the conditions and characteristics of ministry, but does not clearly define it or offer job descriptions.[17] There is ample space for reinterpreting the essence of the text for our contemporary situation. Community, charism and service are the components of this facet of the Christian's response. There are no sacred places, no specially sacred persons; rather all believers are to be the "living stones" offering spiritual sacrifices to God through Jesus.[18] We have little of structures and more of the principle of the apostolic tradition even in the later pastoral epistles.[19] Likewise, the gift of leading the community is one of the many services in the church, and is described by Paul rather than being given a special name (1 Th 5:12).

Another interesting phenomenon is the variety of coworkers collaborating and serving with Paul and others. There seems to be an extension of service and an interest in utilizing the full potential of each person. Some ministers are public in their service, such as evangelists, some are key figures in the local church, others have an itinerant quality about their life and ministry. Not only is there a broad view of ministry and a variety of specific ministries but some believers are called to a wider sphere of personal influence. The apostles in the early church are examples of this clear missionary orientation. The prophets were another special group in the early church who challenged and encouraged the community in its Christian response. Their preaching often led to a presiding at the Eucharist and to the exercise of leadership in the church.[20] Women also had specific roles and frequently exercised a special ministry to women and to other Christians in the early church.

All forms of ministry were a specific response to the call of Jesus to his disciples. Ministry itself was a proclamation of God's action in Jesus and a living out of Jesus' words of compassion, justice and love. This grounding in Christ gives a solid foundation to the ministry of his followers. However, rather than slavish imitation of Christ, there was an ability in the ecclesial community to proclaim the good news in new ways and in new forms. The image of Jesus as minister is expansive, the work of Jesus bridges earthly and heavenly realities. The New Testament suggests that our ministry be affected by the Risen Lord whom we know in the scripture and experience in our own lives. The Risen Lord unites all humankind but especially the community of believers.[21] This principle of unity among the faithful because of the life-giving function of the Christ is a reality that can enhance the varieties of ministers today. Gift or charism and a baptismal commitment to service seem to characterize the early church as we know it through the scriptures. Bishops, priests, and offices as we understand them are far more developed today than in the apostolic tradition. Even limited definitions of deacons and bishops are absent in the documents of the apostolic church; broad descriptions of the "generic occupation of service" are our heritage.[22] "Flexible" and "charismatic" come to mind when we think of communities and the early church, although there are variations in emphasis in the Gentile and Palestinian based communities. Ministry is adapted to changing circumstances while maintaining a focus on gospel values. It is truly the activity of the Spirit in the followers and co-workers.

The communal dimension of ministry is significant in the New Testament period. The community understands baptism as entrance into ministry and believes that faith must necessarily be translated into action. Charisms arise out of the community for the good of the community. Some charisms are given for the building of the community itself, others extend the community beyond itself. There is a witnessing to the presence of Christ within the community with an appreciation that the fulness of his life is still in the future. There is a celebration remembering Christ's death and resurrection in the Eucharist; there is a proclamation of the word and of the Christian life which is a sign to the believer and non-believer. Christ is within the Christian; the Christian is in Christ. In faith Christians believe that Christ continues to live and act through the ministry of his followers. These biblical insights can encourage ministers today who are looking for spontaneity, new forms and a universal perspective in their development of ministry. The common insight of early Christians is that belief is expressed in the service of others. This service is characterized by diversity in the ministry itself and in the ministering person. All members of the church are responsible for meeting the needs and continuing the life of the community.

If the New Testament identifies a diversity of ministries within the context of the believing community, it also reflects a very dynamic portrayal of church. The community or church experience was intimately related to the daily life of the Christian. The early church provided a context for ministry since believers were encouraged to assess needs and utilize their gifts for the growth of the community. The needs of the church at any given period of time suggest ministries as well as ministers. In the truly Catholic experience of church today there are different local communities, with different needs, offering different assessments and suggesting different solutions regarding pastoral ministry. This provides a rich source of reflection on our identity as church and a variety of models of ministry and ministers that is very similar to the early church period.

The Ecclesial Dimension Of Ministry

If ministry emerges within the ecclesial context, the images of the church are meant to be inspiring, challenging and realistic. The images of church invite and encourage all the baptized to act on behalf of others and in response to human need. The hierarchical image of church was de-emphasized by the Second Vatican Council and the image of church as the People of God emerged. Church is more often described now as a community of believers, a sacrament to the world, a servant and a herald. The family and discipleship models focus on relationships and ministry and are inviting exciting theological reflection. This perspective in our understanding of church grounds the ecclesial dimensions of our spirituality in relationships that grow and change. It also testifies to the rhythms of life which elicit different responses of service within the community. These models lived out on an adult level help us to articulate our experience of commitment as a form of discipleship among equals. Our ecclesiology influences the shape of ministry. A restrictive view of church leads to a restrictive and controlling view of ministry. An expansive and dynamic view of church results in the emergence of ministry in creative and "non-institutionalized" forms. This view enables Christians to contribute as members of the church in ways consistent with their competencies, experience and interests. It also offers hope to the many over-burdened priestly ministers who can now rethink their own ministry in relation to the emergence of a new breed of dedicated Christians.

Questions of effectiveness, service to the world, and the development of the inner life of the church suggest different responses as our vision of church changes. However the temptation to maintain former structures and mentalities prevails. The transformational presence of Christ needs to be experienced widely within the church community. Church officials are challenged to be servants of the church, not servants of the institution, and to respond as Jesus would, rather than in the interests of law and structural preservation.[23] This concretely means that we as church believe that all members, leaders and followers, are inspired by the Spirit, and that we begin to act on that belief. Our times and its needs are suggesting a realignment of church life and a reevaluation of structures and ministry if we are to offer some hope for the future. The church provides the context for ministry and ministry is an expression of who we are as church. There is an evolution in ecclesiology taking place at this time, and this promises the emergence of a more viable and vital spirituality for the future.

Ministry is the expression of our spirituality as baptized Christians. Ministry is understood in light of the New Testament foundation and an understanding of church. However, ministry today has many dimensions to it because of current needs and because of the perspective of the person offering the Christian service. It is to these aspects that we now turn.

Varieties Of Ministry Within The One Spirituality

Ministry may be defined narrowly or broadly, and it has been observed that when everything is considered ministry, ministry fades away.[24] While ministry is for all the baptized, there are, according to O'Meara, characteristics that constitute the nature of ministry, namely, "(1) doing something; (2) for the advent of the kingdom; (3) in public; (4) on behalf of the Christian community; (5) which is a gift received in faith, baptism and ordination; and which is (6) an activity with its own limits and identity within a diversity of ministerial actions."[25]

There are also other classifications of ministry according to Bernard Cooke fundamental for church life: "(1) Christians who form community, (2) ministers of the word, (3) ministers to human needs, (4) ministers of God's judgment, (5) ministers of sacrament."[26] These characteristics can describe priests, religious and laity in the church today. Ministry makes explicit the kingdom proclaimed by Jesus. This kind of service is for each baptized Christian, and it necessitates a harmony and unity of ministries in the community. While ministries emerge from our spirituality and ecclesiology and are associated with activity, they are not activism. Each authentic ministry results from a reflective awareness of the mystery of Christ as presented in the gospels and developed in the tradition. When there is a central focus, ministries can change and evolve so that they continue to be gracious, responsible and authentic.

Christian service is characterized by a servant style, sensitivity, and discernment. Public Christian ministry goes beyond official ministries. Christian service to the socially impoverished, healing, teaching, preaching, community leadership, might happen within the small foundational church or basic ecclesial community. But it happens because the Spirit is leading us to ministry. Service results from Christian awareness and belief, and is perceived as such by others. This aspect of ministry underscores the importance of a vibrant, reflective community of faith which is not only alive to the presence of God but can let his presence permeate its life and decision-making.

Other aspects of ministry include ministry of word and of sacraments, with its counterpart of witnessing by word and life, by sign and celebration. In all these aspects the ministers themselves are drawn by a vision and a goal. They see and are in touch with the deepest realities of life so that power becomes influence and weakness strength. Prophetic judgments are made by such persons, judgments that challenge, confront, comfort, or affirm as a result of the discernment process. These aspects of a person's ministry are grounded in contemplation, in caring, compassion and in the tradition which identifies the parameters of Christian identity. Christian ministry thus engages the total person and is not simply a task. It is outreach emanating from the center, Christ, in response to human and spiritual needs.

Spirituality Of Ministry
  As A Response To Need

The question of need often clarifies ministry for us. Needs in the 1980s and '90s take on the tenor of our times and reflect our culture and our concerns. These needs are experienced within the church and within the world. The Christian minister is at the service of both and is called upon to invite to ministry those who can meet these local, national and global needs. Within the church we are concerned about the rights of the Christian community to the sacraments, particularly the Eucharist, the education of adults in the faith, justice for women, the divorced, minorities, inactive priests. Nowadays, we emphasize conversion in leadership styles for those in leadership positions, the negative effects of maternalism and paternalism, the rights and responsibilities of laity, the healing of factions and recognition of the value of dissent, the obliteration of sexism and a renewed commitment to collaborative models of ministry.

In our world today the issues surfacing include social justice, the restoration of human dignity, individual rights to employment, opportunity, privacy, direction of one's life, a Christian influence in political spheres, cultural life and media, peace, and environmental issues. Our concerns encompass nuclear arms, unjust trade relations, oppressive regimes, terrorism, abuse of human rights, sinful social structures and governments. These concerns will shape ministry in the community of faith. Unless these needs are addressed, Christian ministry will be perceived as exclusive and unrelated to the real world of daily life.

This period in our Vatican II church is ripe for rethinking how we express ourselves as church. It is a search for significance in a time of crisis and transition. Many of the people in ministry are involved in the search for significance and are identifying new needs in themselves. The needs revolve around three focuses, the minister, the ministry and collaborative ministry.

For *the person in ministry*, the emerging emphasis is on the life of the minister, "being" as complementary to "doing", self-anchoring rather than role identity. Free time, reflection and prayer are increasingly necessary for persons who want to be more aware of themselves and more integrated in their approach to life. There is also a desire to exude a healthy involvement in life, to seek challenges and to take risks if we are to continue in our work. However most professional ministers were trained in a very different model of personal identity and so reeducation in areas of personal growth is a real need.

The ministry itself suggests issues to be addressed. Ministry is most frequently to persons in need and because of these circumstances can be draining, lead to fatigue, depression and a decrease in resiliency in the person providing the service. Furthermore, in a better informed church and society, where questioning is more acceptable, people can be more cynical, more critical and less accepting of authority, which makes ministry a new kind of challenge. Effective ministry is difficult because of the integrating skills necessary. How do we make sense out of cultural data, ecclesial tradition, personal abilities, diverse and sometimes conflicting needs? Furthermore, priests in particular are perceived to be masters of all ministries rather than ordained to a particular ministry, encouraging unrealistic expectations. Ministry is making new demands on the minister. Time must now be spent in learning how to deal with conflict and criticism, pluralism and dissent, integrating knowledge and experience and recognizing unrealistic demands. Even success is being redefined.

Finally, the renewed emphasis on *collaboration in ministry* is causing pressure and is suggesting new kinds of concern. Traditional ministries are complemented by other full time services, causing all of us to rethink responsibilities and reassess limitations. The expansion and diversification of ministry is contributing to role conflict and a shifting emphasis on the part of laity, religious and priests. There is an increasing lack of control on the part of structural leaders as numbers of laity and women in ministry increase. Diversity, competency, power, decision-making, shared responsibility, are just some of the issues being addressed. For persons who were trained to self-sufficiency and clear identification of roles, the movement towards collaboration with persons who have different background, education, experience and perceptions of church can be difficult and frustrating. The need for communication skills, dialogue, good self-concept, flexibility, mutual respect and creativity becomes increasingly evident. Each person involved in ministry is continuously identifying strengths and limitations as well as experiencing the urgency of working in new ways with new people.

The future of ministry is filled with excitement as ministerial responsibilities shift from church officials to the believing community. Attitudes are changing and eventually structures will be transformed. The exercise of leadership will be more facilitating, participatory and mutually challenging. Ministry will increasingly be lay ministry; it will be specialized and collaborative, ecumenical and socially significant. These changes will demand a spirituality that is strong and life-giving. Our spirituality may indeed be the decisive factor determining our effectiveness in ministry and our sense of personal fulfillment.

A Spirituality Of Wholistic Integration

A spirituality of the dedicated Christian is expressed in ministry. However, in addressing the issue of ministry, our concern is for effective ministry consistent with gospel values and our ecclesial identity. In order to pursue the idea of effectiveness, we will identify several areas of movement from ineffectiveness to effectiveness and then focus on some integrating points for the minister.

Several serious observations have been made in regard to priestly ministry and the attitudes of religious and priests.

As previously noted in this text (see Chapter 2, Endnote 1), many priests, after twenty-five years in the priesthood, are hesitant to recommend the priesthood to others. These priestly ministers who were exhausted and plagued with varying degrees of burnout were also perceived as unsuitable role models, incapable of attracting others to embrace their life-style. The lack of healthy human models was also seen as a source of stress for the ministers themselves. Furthermore, "Priests and religious not only admit but seem to revel in their spiritual impoverishment, in their wounded state, in their readiness to accept a passive stance to the Spirit because of their own lack of strength."[27]

To move from ineffectiveness in these areas to effectiveness requires a shift in emphasis. All those involved in ministry in the community whether they be religious, priests or laity, must be models of health and wholeness for the community. This will demand a renewed emphasis on all dimensions of personal life and growth. We are challenged to study those among us who exhibit high levels of health and achievement. These peak performers are not only healthy but socially satisfied and fulfilled. There is a sense of well-being, self-esteem, self-caring and an inner-directedness.[28] A phenomenon called "flow state" has been described. It is the "wholistic sensation present when we act with total involvement . . . the state in which action flows upon action according to an internal logic which seems to need no conscious intervention on our part. We experience it as a unified flowing from one moment to the next."[29]

Another aspect of ineffectiveness focuses on rigidity and work fixation. Rigid rules, applied without consideration of persons or situations, contribute to alienation and burnout.[30] Also attitudes toward work can be restrictive. Is all of our life composed of what we *have* to do or do we have an ability to choose what we *want* to do?[31] If we are fixated

Developing A Spirituality For Ministers 45

on work, resiliency fails and we have the tendency to go too far in situations of ministry. Stress in work is also attributed to uncertainty and lack of control. These can cause immobilization as well as frustration.

These negative components of life can be turned around only by a radical reorientation of attitudes regarding work, change and rules. It is often suggested that we give ourselves permission to be less than perfect in a period of transition as we test new ideas, attitudes and approaches.[32] Likewise, an appreciation of leisure and a fully satisfying life will counteract the fixation on work-related activities and even transform our work attitudes. Furthermore, an appreciation of shared responsibility, which also means shared burdens, will move us to more creative and effective approaches.

Finally, the paralyzing effects of stress need attention. Can we complement the hassles of life with uplifting, relational and wholistic experiences? Can we examine our approach to ministry? Is our work never done? Are results hard to identify? Does repetitiveness, people's expectations, or working with the same people get us down? Are we drained by people in need, by people who are looking for "strokes" rather than solid spiritual food? Do we need to minister behind a mask, one that never permits us to be angry or to fail?[33]   Life's stresses will also be present as well as stresses in ministry.

However a turnaround is always possible. We can associate with positive people and choose friends who are fulfilled and uplifting. We can be honest with ourselves and accept responsibility for our lives and our choices. We can accept stress within reasonable limits, clarify our roles and create a spirit of confidence in our ability to meet demands creatively and effectively. Finding energy again results from creative relationships and endeavors, paying attention to thoughts, fantasies and dreams as well as meditation.[34] Ineffectiveness can be transformed into effectiveness when we identify the stumbling blocks in ourselves and develop alternatives.

For the Christian minister, there are several significant integrating points. Because of our faith commitment we have resources unavailable to purely secular persons. Our religious tradition emphasizes contemplative prayer which fosters and develops our interior vision. Meditation and centering prayer have the side effects of a deep relaxation response. We also have a rich tradition of discernment which enhances our decision-making ability. Recent church teaching underscores an appreciation of the good things of life. Our church life consists of community relationships and a hopeful vision regarding the world. Our present focus in ministry is on facilitating ministry in others and a renewed appreciation of gospel values. Within the Christian experience are all the ingredients for a fulfilling and satisfying life. Our spirituality, which is the lived expression of our faith, can lead us to an effectiveness appropriate for the Christian.

Furthermore, we are committed to fostering a healthy orientation in our Christian lives. Rather than speaking of simplicity, we are striving for simplification in our life and ministry. We are recognizing that ministers also need to be ministered to, and we are beginning to personally accept the reality of mutual ministry. We are more comfortable with weakness and limitations, knowing that these do not necessarily mean ineffectiveness. We are developing within ourselves emotional maturity and an inner strength. We are learning about transitions and accepting crises as a part of our existence. We are creating supportive environments, developing long term goals and appreciating the various rhythms of our lives. In all these aspects, we are enlarging our sense of identity and allowing it to evolve over time. We are committing ourselves to a spacious way of living and a gracious way of serving. We are cultivating attitudes of care, concern, courage and collaboration. These qualities are potentially the integrating points that will enable us to process all that penetrates our consciousness from the church and the world. It is our faith — accepted and lived — that consistently moves us to greater effectiveness in the service of others.

    A spirituality for the ministering person is essential for this decade in which we live. Spirituality today searches out new areas as well as reminding us of the traditional ones. It expresses itself consistently in ministry as in New Testament times, and inserts itself within the framework of the church. Ministry becomes effective and enhances personal growth and fulfillment if we recognize and utilize the points of integration open to us. In fact, a spirituality well lived and understood provides the integrating focus for the Christian and fosters our striving for the excellence and effectiveness of the gospel.

Chapter 4

Enhancing Our Approaches To Ministry

Ministry in the latter part of the last century is complex and arouses in the most dedicated people a concern for present effectiveness and future relevancy. Part of the concern, as we have seen, is the relatively new phenomenon of burnout which takes its toll among the best in any given profession. Effectiveness in ministry is now being approached as part of a total way of life inextricably linked to a sense of personal fulfillment, and we are searching for a spirituality that will enable us to experience that Christian life to the full. Chapter 3 dealt with these points on a more theoretical level. In this chapter, I will suggest some concrete ways of avoiding burnout in its early stages, so that professional ministers can enhance both their life and their ministry. An initial step will be an emphasis on our acceptance of the problem of stress and burnout with its implications for church personnel. We must also identify the special need among professional Christian ministers. Then work itself will be explored with some directions emerging from contemporary business practice that can enhance ministry. Finally, we will suggest some practical approaches in the form of aids, support systems and helps towards integration.

Acceptance Of The Impact Of Stress

In order to address the problem of the kind of stress that leads to burnout in certain predisposed individuals, it would be well for each of us to remind ourselves again that the problem actually exists. Admitting the seriousness of stress in our lives, especially in the lives of professional ministers, is the first step towards finding a solution. An untoward amount of friction and anxiety depletes our resources, vitality and energy. Furthermore, when burnout exists, we usually unwittingly continue along the self-destructive path.[1] Increased pressure can lead to a decrease in the quality of our work and our lives if it gets beyond what we can handle. Likewise, it is significant, as we have previously seen, that the burnout associated with work or ministry can result from the situation itself and is not necessarily a function of a person's dispositional inadequacy.[2] This fact has great significance for an individual's ability to maintain self-esteem while dealing with situations of stress. Awareness of the problem of stress also means that we see the negative effects of underchallenge as well as overchallenge, especially for those dedicated to church ministry. In these situations, the encouragement of the individual to take responsibility for their lives, to act rather than to deny, to change rather than accept, is paramount. Burnout was unheard of when options were few. Because of the many opportunities and the high expectations, we can easily begin to move along the path to burnout. Awareness of this possibility is a first step towards the prevention or resolution of the problem.

In extensive conversations with dedicated women and men,[3] I was constantly impressed with the level of awareness of the problems associated with burnout and with the insights offered that could alleviate the distress. In the post Vatican II church, the conflict caused when people were closed to change, deeply affected professional ministers. Those resisting change can be found among the various vocations in the church, and is particularly distressing when these people should be collaborators. Religious communities, with their lifestyle demands, were a source of conflict and tension for some religious women. Traditional church structures, myths about the identity of religious and laity, change occuring at different rates, differing points of view regarding essentials, being dominated by one's role, a lack of preparation for the new demands of ministry, critical and defensive coworkers and stereotyping were also cited as factors that contribute to the problem. This level of awareness of the situation by so many religious in particular is a first step towards resolution, at least on a personal level.

When we speak about stress and burnout, we are not simply speaking about a scientific or medical entity, but about human resources. For any organization, and for the Christian churches, the loss of the best individuals during this critical period is a serious problem. The issue is being addressed on many levels. Human resource planning is a recently developed form of pastoral planning that many dioceses and religious communities are now utilizing.[4] Behavioral medicine with its emphasis on stress management, the enhancement of personal skills, diet, exercise, and therapy, attests to the value of maintaining and enhancing our human potential and offers some solutions.[5] However, within the ecclesial community, there are particular areas of need. Among these are education for change, assessment of skills and skill transfer to meet new needs and to accommodate to changing rhythms of life, examination of retirement practices and of current policies regarding ordination to the priesthood. Crisis intervention is another need and requires special skills when one is dealing with persons with a strong faith commitment. Other significant concerns include the integration of sexuality into a celibate commitment, dealing with mid-life transitions in this context, a viable means of evaluating professional ministers and the development of support systems and structures for church workers. As we continually identify these and other areas of need we are also taking the initial steps towards the eradication of problem areas. Likewise, as we explore some of the current literature and reflect on secular experience, we see possibilities of their implementation within the church. Let us look briefly at work in the professional sphere.

The Quality Of Work

While it is beyond the scope of this chapter to examine the many recent developments in organizational development and personnel management, we can present some highlights from these interesting areas of research. Consistent emphases emerge in contemporary organizations that include loose supervision, the encouragement of self control and direction in work, the participation of employees in the organization itself, increasing job variety for the individual with the necessary broad job descriptions, innovative approaches in managing people, and an equal concern for productivity and quality of work life.[6]

The focus in many businesses and organizations is on the team approach to job design with the variety, support, and social interaction that it offers. With this team emphasis comes the development of interpersonal training programs, since no group is better than its weakest link.[7] Job satisfaction and employee retention are associated with social contacts within the workplace. These training programs serve the companies in several ways.

We also see increasing interest in job design and redesign, job rotation, planning and forecasting, personal career planning and development.[8] These areas of development are a response to the graying of our population. Effective training should create realistic expectations, be practical, thorough, relevant, develop sophisticated interpersonal skills, enhance knowledge of the bureaucratic structures and suggest ways to work in them. It should also train workers to cope with stress, conflict, uncertainty, change and burnout.[9] Businesses continue to explore the feasibility of reemployment practices which will extend employment beyond the mandatory retirement age and provide options to early retirement.[10] These current business practices have clear implications for church personnel. It is likewise a hopeful sign that some of these approaches are already implemented in certain groups of professional ministers and in some areas within the church.

A final but fascinating area studied by people concerned with business and leadership is the question of feedback as a motivator for change. Schuler identifies ten characteristics of effective feedback and suggests using this process rather than evaluation.[11] There are differences between feedback and evaluation. Feedback is descriptive; it provides individuals with information which they can use in their own evaluation. Evaluations given by others tend to be seen as criticism or judgments on "goodness" or "badness."[12] The feedback technique is a good tool because it describes the work behavior. The description is sufficiently non-threatening for the person to hear and to assess. It keeps the channels of communication open, expects the individual to contribute to the conversation, and offers real possibilities for dialogue and change to occur.

Even a cursory glance at some of the developments in the business world offer potential areas for the Christian minister and church officials to explore. The issues of concern in the work area are issues of concern for the Christian minister. Our motivation and our resources might differ, but fulfillment, growth, and quality are important to both groups. When business is forced to redefine the essence of success, moving away from promotions to a job redesign and other alternatives, can the professional minister and the Christian community do less? We can learn about quality work in the marketplace, from the business community, and its educators. We can adapt and reinterpret these approaches in terms of Christian ministry, perhaps alleviating some of the stressful situations we experience within the church.

While awareness of the problem of stress and burnout is essential for prevention and for treatment, and while the developments in the world of work offer perspectives and reinforcement of some of the directions within the church, there are many practical things we can do to better deal with stress and distress. It is to these suggestions that we now turn.

Approaches And Aids For Growth In Ministry

Our interest in stress and burnout, as well as in the development of a spirituality for the ministering person, is the enhancement of Christian life and an increased effectiveness by professional ministers in their service of others. If stress overwhelms a person, then a considerable amount of effort is necessary to regain control of one's life. Simple efforts like structuring time, marshalling a support system, balancing work and leisure, doing something for someone else, rewarding oneself, and recognizing that no one can care as much as you do about your happiness, are extremely effective.[13] Small changes and responses help. Realistic expectations along with time management and planning are positive steps. The effectiveness of any approach can be measured by a person's openness to new experiences and his or her renewed ability to see the world as a place of discovery.

On a personal level, it is important to take our growth seriously, to feel happy and fulfilled, to have a healthy self image, to give priority time to ourselves, to value what we are doing within the church. This might mean that we do not constantly compare ourselves to others, and that we work against an unhealthy sensitivity. We can also acknowledge our limitations and say we "can't do it." A religious woman, who handled a complicated administrative position within her congregation extremely well, said, "If I am a happy and fulfilled person I will find in my ministry an opportunity for growth and enrichment." The other alternative is the feeling of "being trapped" by the demands of ministry and seeing these demands as "taking away the time I need for myself." Taking care of yourself, having a good sense of space, developing a sense of humor, thinking positive thoughts, listening to affirmation and relishing it, are concrete steps each of us can take to enhance our personal resources. Furthermore, professional ministers need a strong faith in God, a spirituality that balances work and leisure as well as time for prayer if they are to grow in a wholistic way.

Each of us also needs to identify what promotes relaxation for us. Walking, exercise, a comfortable chair, good music, enjoying nature, playing a musical instrument, talking with a friend are all frequently mentioned as reducers of stress. If it is hard for you to relax or to take time for leisure, then initially you will have to "make yourself do it"! Enjoyment and new rhythm in life will come in time.

In regard to ministry itself, there are some concrete steps we can take to reduce stress and to promote effectiveness. Be prepared for the job you are doing. If further education is needed, then plan on obtaining it, while not underestimating your abilities. Talking over problems with associates, making use of specialists in the area to periodically review problems, study of the issues or aspects of ministry in which you are involved, taking breaks from the routine and the environment are healthy and effective approaches. When you have made a significant contribution or achieved something of value, take the time to enjoy your accomplishment before moving on to something else. Likewise, it is important to be open to professional help in coping with stress, or to develop good time-management techniques. Another person's perspective is sometimes the critical difference in understanding ourselves and providing the impetus for change. Some extremely effective people find that it is helpful to them personally to give workshops, to plan programs for others, and to get involved in continuing education. Forcing oneself to study the issues and to challenge others in positive approaches also assists the provider of the service. Suggestions given by people who were close to burnout were: "make a specific effort to do something for someone else," "force yourself to be actively involved," "distance yourself for a while, if necessary." A real commitment to professional and spiritual reading expands our perspective, and a timely sabbatical can rejuvenate even the most weary among us. In fact, a quality sabbatical experience can frequently prevent job change for reasons of stress, as well as give the individual a unique opportunity to plan for the next phase of his or her life. Religious communities are increasingly open to discerning personal needs as they affect an individual's effectiveness in ministry. This approach will not only assist the persons involved in the process but also contribute to the development of healthy models among professional ministers in the church.

Support Systems

One of the most significant aids to the avoidance of burnout is the development of support systems. We can identify these support systems on an individual, professional, and institutional level. Their effectiveness is widely lauded by people in the professions and in ministry. The most frequently mentioned support to people in ministry is a good friend. A friend is "vital," "a must," "a sounding board," "a person to share mutual concerns or problem areas." "Being able to talk with someone," is the best support system, while "being a friend" enables the support to be mutual and builds a system of friendship relationships. There are numerous studies on professional women that consistently identify the stress involved in their career advancement and in their working with people. However, it is also consistently mentioned that women tend to have a wealth of human supports that enable them to cope exceedingly well.[14]

Professional Support Groups

Professional support systems help in burnout prevention. Many of the helping professions — among them, nursing, counselling, social work, law enforcement, teaching, and clergy — acknowledge and utilize support groups. Sometimes these support systems go beyond the place of work to a community, a city, a diocese. Persons in similar professions or ministries can share the joys and frustrations of their work life and acknowledge the importance of peer support. These groups can also provide educational opportunities and problem solving sessions, thereby increasing skills and preventing avoidable stress. For many of these groups, a significant contributing factor is the sharing among men and women in a given profession. With the emphasis on team ministry and collaborative models of ministry, these exchanges can be particularly helpful for church personnel. This sharing might diffuse the stereotype that "men handle the problems of others better than women," as competent professionals speak openly about themselves, their problems and their frustrations. These mixed groups also give women and men the opportunity to discover the kind of affirmation that is significant for women and for men. The quality of any support system relates to the ability of the participants to reflect on what happened and why, and to use the group as a support, not a crutch.

The Place Of Institutions As A Support For Ministers

Institutions themselves provide a framework of support but often arouse ambivalent feelings. Within the ministerial context, institutions "can help but can also crush"; they can be "the cause of problems and at times a very good support system"; "many institutions seem to be stressful places to work when they try to provide quality service, and coordinate multiple activities." On the positive side, institutions provide the opportunity of contact with others in the same field, sustain the minister, and often implement prayer and ministry support groups. Religious communities and dioceses provide retreats, and often call together specialized groups, providing opportunities for dialogue and collaboration. Institutions are a part of our lives and can be forces for good. Church institutions can be burdensome, though, when restrictions on certain leadership positions force individuals to accept jobs because they are religious, not because of competence and interest. This occurs most frequently when there are too few people in religious communities to service the institution. Structures, in such cases, need to be revitalized so that the institution can again serve by more creatively exploring its role in the church and world. We might mention here that there is a change in our expectation of some institutions, as indicated by this commonly heard exhortation: "Let us focus on the community aspect where we experience the love, support, and encouragement of the person." Institutions can provide unique opportunities for growth because of the resources available to them. They can foster creativity on many levels by the style of leadership they foster in their administrators. Structural change will result in most organizations when persons or small groups live out and implement their commitment to change. Gradually, then, the old structures will be rendered less useful. Finally, organizations and institutions often bring together very disparate groups within the church and are the meeting ground for priests, religious and laity of many different backgrounds. "I would like to know what dedicated laity are thinking," say many religious. Institutional settings can foster dialogue among vocational groups, and complement what is occurring on a personal and professional level.

Sound support systems set up a network of communication and mutual concern. When they function well, they provide ready listeners, technical and emotional support, and challenge. They are a social reality that can truly enhance our effectiveness in ministry by constantly building self-esteem while suggesting alternatives to problems and issues. They will prevent the stress that leads to burnout when they are utilized well.

Our twofold emphasis, finding personal fulfillment and enhancing effectiveness in ministry, leads us again to the concept of integration. As Christian persons we are vitally interested in total commitment while not "wearing out." We are seeking an integrated approach to life where the service of others and the enjoyment of life are seen as aspects of worship. We attempt to draw upon our personal and religious strengths so that the fulness of life promised by the Lord will become more of reality. In order for this to happen, each one of us must reflect on our own personal stories, and our own responses to situations. Could we not ask, When did I feel most myself, most fulfilled and happy? When did I experience the fulness of my potential in my personal life and in my ministry? Then we could identify the components of those experiences and the aspects of integration. For many people, reflection, leisure, a good conversation, and enjoyable activity, are closely connected to their most fulfilling moments in ministry. Working at work does not necessarily bring about the quality of work or of life that we desire, while a well rounded life experience often does. Personal relaxation, hobbies, vacations, retreats, are ways to complement the demands of ministry if we choose these pursuits wisely. For example, if we are constantly involved with people, a solitary pursuit can enhance our personality, and our ability to relax. If we must work within strict rules and structures, then a complementary, and perhaps spontaneous leisure activity would serve us well. For many of us, we are speaking about a conversion on many levels and a discerning of new priorities when we discuss the integration of life and ministry. But is this not what it means to be a Christian in a changing but exciting world?

In the last analysis, each individual involved in ministry within the Church must take personal responsibility for his or her life. Friends and spiritual directors can suggest, support, and challenge. However, each one of us must know ourselves sufficiently well to understand our potential, our strengths and our limitations. With this knowledge, and a commitment to growth, choices can be made to enhance and develop our personal selves, and consequently, our ministerial effectiveness.

CHAPTER 5

JESUS: A Model For All Ecclesial Ministers

In the previous chapters, we focused on some concerns and issues regarding personal fulfillment and effectiveness in ministry. We also identified the components of a spirituality for ministers, and reflected on helpful approaches that could contribute to a more integrated Christian life. Now we turn our attention to our biblical roots, and to the earliest gospel tradition. A rereading of scripture from the vantage point of ministry, will enable us to discover the rhythms of ministry as well as the attitudes toward ministry of Jesus and the disciples. We will also assess the responses and reactions of Jesus and the disciples to difficult situations. The Gospel of Mark[1] offers many examples of ministry and suggests what constitutes effectiveness. It challenged the Christians in the 60s and 70s of the first century; it offers some significant perspectives for Christians in the '80s and '90s of the twentieth century.

When we think of Mark's Gospel, two themes quickly come to mind, namely, Jesus as the suffering Messiah, and discipleship. Throughout the Markan narrative the focus is clearly on the person Jesus, a very dynamic and human portrayal for Mark. From the outset of his ministry, Jesus calls others to follow him as disciples, and to be involved in his mission of proclaiming the presence of the Kingdom of God in word and deed. In this chapter we will be concerned about the mission of Jesus, and will examine the Gospel of Mark from the perspective of this involvement in ministry. Initially, the gospel portrays the preparation for, and call to ministry, in Jesus and the disciples. Then Mark offers a glimpse of the actual activity of Jesus which serves as the basis for his theology of ministry, and he also presents the varied responses of others to Jesus' work. Following this presentation the author identifies the attitudes of the disciples and their ministerial effectiveness. Finally, the gospel of Mark stimulates our reflection on the implications of the ministry of Jesus and his disciples for contemporary Christian ministers. The gospel insights reinforce some of the approaches we have discussed in our treatment of the topic of personal fulfillment and effectiveness in ministry.

The Call To Ministry

In Mark's account, Jesus begins his ministry only after a special preparation for it. Scripture announces the sending of a messenger in the words of the prophet Isaiah (Mk 1:2-3). This messenger, John, preaches forgiveness of sins and baptizes those who come to him in the wilderness. However, both scripture and John prepare the way of the Lord. John points to the one who comes after him, the one who baptizes with the Holy Spirit (1:7-8). The activity of the precursor prepares for the appearance and the ministry of Jesus, whom John later baptizes in the Jordan. A progression takes place in this gospel: Jesus, disciples, Christians. What is said of one is implied for the others.

Then Mark establishes the context of Jesus' ministry in the baptismal scene and the temptations, which point to the unique dimension in which Jesus acts (1:9-13). After this initiation Jesus begins his preaching of the gospel of God and his calling of disciples. The beginning of the gospel sets a dynamic in motion; the preparation for ministry is through the word of scripture, the call of another, and the word of the Father: "This is my beloved Son" (1:11). Only after his baptism and his struggle in the desert is the Lord ready to proclaim his message and to call others to follow him. The emphasis early in chapter one of Mark is on the spiritual preparations for ministry.

When Jesus calls others, he presents them with a task to accomplish. To Simon and Andrew, he says, "Follow me and I will make you fishers of men" (1:17). Discipleship implies a task, for to be "fishers of men" is to prepare others to hear the word of the Lord, and to gather the community of the faithful. Later, Jesus names the Twelve as his companions, and they are sent out to preach and to cast out demons (3:14-15). The call to enter into a relationship with the Lord is again connected with service. In Mark 8:34, Jesus speaks to all those who would follow him and challenges them to self-denial and the acceptance of suffering. Disciples live out this dimension of self-sacrifice concretely in the service of others.

The very fact that Jesus calls disciples and expects involvement from them is a strong statement in Mark. From the beginning Jesus invites others to serve with him. He seeks collaborators and links ministry with the call of those who follow him. Likewise, as the Markan narrative unfolds, Jesus and the disciples interact, form deep bonds and a sense of mutual commitment. Ministry is not portrayed as individualistic in this gospel. Rather Jesus gathers those who will serve with him and together as a group they respond in service to others. In these few episodes, Mark demonstrates that Jesus and the disciples see in their call a significant commitment to ministry, a point we are emphasizing in our times, and a point we examined in our understanding of spirituality in chapter 3.

The Ministry Of Jesus

Mark grounds ministry for Jesus and for the disciples in baptism and/or call, showing his conviction that service is an essential component of a Christian's response. Likewise Mark sees Jesus as the one believers are to follow. He therefore perceives Jesus as providing the model for all Christian ministry. Jesus' involvement includes a traditional commitment to teaching, proclamation and healing, with the added components of controversy and challenge. With this perspective in mind, we will examine the ministry of Jesus in terms of its key activities and central ideas.

In Mark's portrayal of Jesus, he frequently uses the designation of "teacher." The ministry of Jesus does in fact involve a considerable amount of *teaching*. At times the teaching takes place in the synagogue on special days like the Sabbath (1:21). In other situations, Jesus is simply available to the large crowds that follow him and gather around to hear his word (2:13; 4:1). In his response to persons and to the crowds, Jesus demonstrates a consistent ability to exercise a ministry in response to need and not necessarily one of his own choosing (10:1). Hearers perceive the teaching of Jesus as new (2:13), and he often speaks at great length and in parables (4:11). While Jesus teaches a message that people could understand, according to Mark, acceptance depends on the faith of the listener (4:11-12; 12:12).

In his teaching ministry, Jesus is aware of individuals and their needs and responds to them. He also leaves a place if people are not ready for his message (6:5-6). Furthermore, he is frequently moved by very human motivation, such as his pity for the crowd because they are like sheep without a shepherd (6:34). In this instance, although Mark explicitly states that Jesus teaches them many things, little is known of the content of his teaching. However, people do find the message difficult to accept in its entirety, and this eventually leads to his betrayal and the death of the Son of Man (9:31). Opposing groups like the Pharisees challenge the message of Jesus, but he uses the accepted sources of scripture to emphasize his point (12:24). Likewise he offers new ideas in his sharing with the disciples (13:2; 8:31), and gives special explanations to them (4:34). Finally, the teaching of Jesus instills a confidence in others (13:9-11) because of the confidence and authority of Jesus himself (13:20-23, 31). He emphatically states that his words will never pass away. In his teaching ministry, Jesus utilizes a variety of opportunities to teach, responds to needs in service, stimulates opposing views, and deepens the understanding of his followers. He is concerned about effectiveness and growth in ministry, as we are.

Proclamation of God's word is another essential component of the ministry of Jesus. He proclaims the good news of the kingdom (1:14; 2:2) throughout the whole region (1:38). In fact, Jesus is not tied to any one place but preaches and ministers throughout Galilee (1:39), the Gerasene territory (5:1), Judea, and the Jordan region (10:1), displaying throughout the qualities of an itinerant preacher (7:31). Furthermore, no one is excluded from hearing the good news. It will even be proclaimed to the Gentiles before the end times (13:10).

Jesus not only verbally proclaims the good news in preaching, but he visibly portrays it in his other forms of ministry, namely teaching and healing. Thus Mark sees proclamation as a distinctive ministry as well as an underlying component in all the activities of Jesus. For ministers today, every service provides an opportunity to proclaim the good news. Likewise, we are visible signs of what we proclaim, just as Jesus and the disciples were.

Perhaps it is the *healing* ministry of Jesus the miracle-worker which is the most compelling portrait in the gospel. Mark incorporates the healings and exorcisms into the broader dimensions of Jesus' ministry. For example, healing frequently follows preaching (1:38). However, in the miracle stories Mark also demonstrates the unique ability of Jesus to meet needs and to teach at the same time. In the instance of the cure of the leper, Mark notes the human element of compassion (1:41-42) as Jesus touches the person and heals him. However, Jesus also respects the traditions of his people in this episode when he asks the leper to show himself to the priest. In a very moving incident, Jesus asks the disciples to call Bartimaeus over to him, making it easy for the beggar to be touched by the Lord (10:49). To those who have seemingly little to recommend them, Jesus offers his healing gift. In his cure of the paralytic, Jesus offers both physical healing and spiritual forgiveness (2:1-12). He thus meets the deeper desires of the person and teaches others to be sensitive to *unspoken* needs. Because Jesus is effective in his ministry, curing many as the summary statements indicate, all who have afflictions attempt to press towards him in order to touch him (3:10). In these accounts, service leads to more demands for service. In order to meet these demands, Jesus involves others in ministry according to their gifts and competencies. This portrayal of Jesus, inviting others to share in ministry, is a useful model for the church today.

While Jesus' healing is extremely effective — the deaf-mute speaks plainly (7:35), and the blind man sees clearly (8:22-25) — Jesus significantly moves away from the spectacular and even occasionally cures before the crowd has a chance to gather (9:25). He also speaks of secrecy in regard to these powerful acts because for Mark, Jesus' identity encompasses more than his wonder-working ability (5:43). As a healer, Jesus embodies appealing human qualities and is effective in meeting the various needs of the people of his time. He is also perceptive in assessing real needs, and in affirming traditional ministers in their role.

However, Jesus' involvement with others of necessity stirs up *controversy* and opposition to his ministry (2:1-3:6; 7:1-23; 11:1-33). Jesus seems to expect difficulties and often confronts the attitudes of his opponents. He has the courage of his convictions, speaking with strength and authority (11:29). At the end of one of the controversy sections of Mark's gospel, Jesus grieves that the opponents' minds are closed against him (3:5). While he stirs up opposition by his challenging remarks (12:38), he is also sensitive to the personal ramifications of such confrontations.

In this dimension of his ministry, Jesus again utilizes scriptural foundations for his response. But he consistently reinterprets the tradition for his audience (10:3). In his argument with the Pharisees, the opposition party of the day, Jesus forcefully defends his own ministry (7:1-13; 8:11-13). Inappropriate attitudes and essential issues provide the stimulus and content for the controversy episodes. Insignificant issues do not warrant the attention of Jesus in his ministry. This point reinforces the need for evaluating priorities and discerning the essentials in ministry, as we discussed in an earlier chapter.

Finally, the ministry of Jesus is one of *challenge* to others, a challenge to grow and change. Jesus speaks quite openly in this gospel (8:2), and in regard to specific issues, he clearly identifies the place of the temple in the life of the community (11:4) and its importance for all peoples (11:17). When the disciples appear concerned about their own ministry, he singles out prayer as the essential element for effectiveness (9:28-29). Furthermore, even though the disciples and Jesus have a deep mutual relationship, he offers no empty promises to his supporters (10:40), but impresses them with the rudiments of his message. In a moving incident with the little children, Jesus invites those closest to him to expand their views and perspectives, serving with love, tenderness, and openness to all (10:14). Perhaps, also in this act of Jesus' acceptance of the little ones is an underlying challenge to the community of Mark regarding church membership.

Jesus presents challenges to all whom he encounters, but he reserves his most poignant ones for the disciples. Peter is rebuked, "get behind me Satan," because he is judging by false standards (8:32-33). Jesus tells his followers that they must expect suffering and that the greatest must serve. Jesus also consistently invites the disciples to grow in their faith, since a strong faith eliminates fear (6:5-6; 4:40) and opens a believer to true knowledge. In addition, Jesus suggests that disciples put everything into perspective by his confronting questions about their personal discussions (9:16, 33).

While Jesus challenges opponents and believers alike, perhaps the greatest challenge is the one Jesus himself faces in full and complete acceptance of his own destiny. In the powerful Gethsemane scene (14:32-42), Jesus in prayer pleads and questions the Father before finally accepting his will. Jesus seems to be moved to the roots of his being, and in this encounter, offers the appropriate attitudes and ultimate response demanded of the Christian. The process of struggle, rather than passive acceptance, is the model the Lord offers to his followers as they struggle to understand their role in the church. These challenges are not lost in our time of transition and crisis.

The ministry of Jesus involves teaching, proclamation,

healing. Controversy and the challenge of others are likewise significant dimensions of Jesus' involvement with people. In the exercise of his ministry, Jesus invites a new response to his person and his message by the way he utilizes the traditional forms of ministry, and the ways he goes beyond them.

Response To The Ministry Of Jesus

While the immediacy and urgency of the ministry of Jesus demands a response, the actual reactions to Jesus differ widely in Mark's narrative. Many, after hearing the message and being touched by the Lord, follow him (2:14; 3:34-35; 10:52). Furthermore, disciples participate in his ministry, teach, proclaim and heal as Jesus does (3:13-16; 6:7, 8, 12, 13, 30, 37; 16:15-20). Mark also makes the point that individuals recognize who Jesus is and acknowledge him in faith (8:27-29; 15:39). His words and acts frequently amaze the bystanders (1:27; 5:20; 7:37; 10:32); his teaching holds others spellbound (1:22; 9:15).

However, the response to the powerful and effective ministry of Jesus is not exclusively positive. There are scores of persons who do not understand Jesus and whose minds are completely closed to him (6:52; 7:18; 8:21; 16:11, 13). He is too much for them (6:3)! In fact, some people ask him to go away from their district for his power is too great (5:17). Others are fearful, and hesitate to question him (6:50; 10:32; 16:8; 9:32). Still others plot against him seeking his destruction (3:6).

Mark vividly portrays the responses to the person and ministry of Jesus as ranging from acceptance and recognition to rejection. Measurable success and approval in ministry is elusive and incomplete for Jesus himself. The lessons in these passages resonate with the current concerns of the professional minister.

The Ministry Of The Disciples

Although the focus has been primarily on the ministry of Jesus in its various forms and on the diversity of response to the ministry, Mark also gives attention to the disciples and their ministry. In the gospel of Mark, Jesus and his disciples spread the good news of the kingdom. Jesus and his disciples teach, heal and proclaim. In fact, the ministry of both Jesus and his disciples is similar in the kind of service they offer and in the itinerant quality of their mission. All that is predicated of the ministry of Jesus is expected of the disciples as well. In addition, Jesus emphasizes several other areas that are significant for the effective ministry of his followers. Generally, Jesus suggests appropriate personal attitudes, and identifies various elements of a Christian lifestyle that are necessary for a commitment to ministry.

Among the attitudes Jesus emphasizes for his disciples in their ministry are an openness to others and a servant quality in their approach. Those who perceive their role as an extension of the ministry of the Lord himself should welcome all: children (9:36-37), the sick, and sinners (2:7). Associations with the outcast and the oppressed, which Jesus valued in his own ministry, are the very associations he challenges the disciples to value (2:17). Furthermore, Jesus suggests to the disciples that their basic approach to ministry be that of people who serve (9:35; 10:42-43). The servant quality is the essential attribute for the disciples of Jesus. Even though special experiences and teachings are theirs, the disciples should be known for their humble service of everyone (9:2, 9; 5:37; 4:10-12).

Another notable quality Jesus frequently suggests for

his followers is an ability to discern priorities. Mark presents an interesting episode to illustrate this point. In chapter six, the gospel presents a rather chaotic scene in which people are coming and going in great numbers, making it impossible for these active ministers to so much as get a bite to eat (6:31). In the midst of this activity, Jesus asks the disciples to come away by themselves to rest a while. They in fact go away to a lonely place. This retreat is a regular custom for Jesus and the disciples, for they frequently withdrew to the desert, the mountain, or the sea, the typical places for solitude and prayer (1:35, 45; 6:32-35, 46). These places, rich in Old Testament imagery, are reminders of roots and tradition. In these passages, Jesus invites the disciples to insure certain rhythms in their ministry. They need to be alone because of the pressing demands of the crowds, as well as for prayer, privacy and mutual support. It is interesting to observe the dynamics of this invitation to pause and to rest a while. In Mark, the suggestion is generally preceded by an account of intense activity, usually preaching, and the performance of a mighty deed. Even though there are extensive demands for service, and an extraordinary pressure from the crowds (1:33; 2:2; 3:9-10; 5:31; 6:31), Jesus suggests a retreat to the disciples. Then after the period of leisure and refreshment, the writer of the gospel portrays a more effective ministry (6:30-56). Although Mark creates the aura of immediacy and of urgency in his writing, he also portrays Jesus as cultivating in his followers the attitudes and qualities essential for a long and effective ministry. Acceptable priorities include not only the needs of others, but also the needs of the disciples themselves.

Jesus emphasizes the importance of faith for his followers. The disciples' ministry is effective when characterized by faith, for Jesus promises that all things are possible with God (10:27). Jesus also gives his word and speaks with authority in regard to the quality of life of those who follow him (10:29-30). However, he realistically points out areas of concern and possible limitations. Lack of prayer is the prime hindrance to effectiveness in ministry (9:28-29), and lack of faith is the real enemy (9:19; 11:24). According to Mark, God freely offers the gift of faith, but the disciples make the choice to grow in faith. Therefore, ministers can set limits to their effectiveness because each person can choose the level and the quality of their response to the Lord. Jesus is straightforward in his demands and in his challenges. He invites his disciples to make growth in faith a real priority and commitment.

Because the disciples are visible witnesses to the people who hear the word they proclaim, Jesus challenges them to reflect on the quality of their witness. The very lifestyle of the followers of Jesus is a component of their ministry, and so he calls them to maintain the spark of enthusiasm, to be salt for one another, and to be at peace (9:50). He also states that they be willing to give up everything, even their lives for one another (10:45), and above all, be willing to suffer for his sake (8:31). Furthermore, Jesus urges forgiveness of one another (11:25), an essential virtue as persons attempt to grow into a community of faith. The lifestyle of the disciples of Jesus is simply a concrete living out of their convictions. It is a sign of hope and gives another level of credibility to the message they proclaim.

Finally, just as Jesus invites disciples to be collaborators in the service of others, he also invites them to cultivate an expansive view of ministry and ministers. When those close to Jesus question the work of a healer outside the group, Jesus is clear in his reply (9:39). He seems able to let go of the control of his ministry, and offers a positive view of the person who casts out demons in his name. He asks the disciples to broaden their horizons and to look favorably upon the intentions and the effectiveness of the ministry of others. How obvious are the challenges to the church today.

Although Jesus and his disciples are in constant demand by persons in need and are portrayed as those who serve, Mark conveys another dimension of ministry in his narrative. In the gospel, he mentions as significant the fact that women follow Jesus and minister to him (15:41). This statement not only testifies to the ministry of women but also to the reality that Jesus is the recipient of the love, care and concern of others. He accepts the services of these people, and in his response provides a model of mutual ministry in the community of faith. Jesus asks his disciples to collaborate with others, to allow others to offer their gifts, and to personally receive the service of others on their behalf. The minister is ministered to, and a community of interdependent people is the result.

While the ministry of the disciples is similar in scope to the ministry of Jesus, the Lord encourages realistic approaches and offers insightful perspectives to enhance the quality of their work. There is a timelessness in the message.

Jesus' Ministry And Ours Today

In reading Mark's gospel from the perspective of ministry, several essential components of ministry emerge. Ministry for Jesus and for the disciples is an integral part of their commitment. This ministry has a very concrete dimension to it as it is vividly portrayed in the teaching, preaching and healing ministry of Jesus. However, while ministry seems to address needs and raise important issues, the minister himself or herself is not always accepted. What was true for Jesus is a reality for the followers of Jesus. The Lord is the paradigm as Mark repeatedly demonstrates. In addition, Jesus emphasizes formative attitudes, as well as the importance of concrete actions, in his challenges to growth. In these interesting portrayals of the involvement of Jesus and his disciples, Mark also suggests some valuable lessons for the Christian minister today. As we explore the implications of Mark's teaching, we will see a reinforcement of some of the positive attitudes we have discussed, that are needed in the stressful situations of our church.

Mark presents a variety of preparations for ministry. In addition to persons who prepare the way of the Lord, the preparations include baptism, temptation, and call. These preparations are spiritual or religious experiences, as opposed to professional development. In this emphasis, the gospel challenges contemporary ministers to assess their preparations for ministry, as well as the kind of influence they exert on others. If ministry is to be Christian ministry, then the spiritual dimensions are extremely significant.

The gospel also identifies a commitment to ministry with the believer's initial response to the call of the Lord. Ministry is, therefore, integral to the Christian life. All Christians are urged to some kind of service of others. Baptism gives us rights and responsibilities. The gospel speaks to an awareness of this commitment, and to an active involvement as well. The current needs of the church, as well as contemporary theology, reinforce this dual perspective, as we have noted in previous chapters.

In Mark, Jesus and his disciples offer service to others. Ministry is not so much the contribution of individuals, as a mutual effort in service by a believing community. Today we give serious consideration to intervocational ministry, and collaboration in ministry. This resonates with the biblical tradition and leads to greater effectiveness in times of special need.

Mark focuses on traditional ministries in his portrayal of the activities of Jesus. However, he always inserts

Jesus: A Model For All Ecclesial Ministers 75

elements of newness, or challenges others to continual growth. In today's church, Christians are asked to consider traditional areas of service, but to approach these with new attitudes. In addition, there is room for a ministry of prophetical confrontation as in the time of Jesus. Challenges might be offered in terms of structures and restricted ministries when community needs might suggest new alternatives.

Mark points to the involvement of Jesus and the disciples with a variety of people. Opponents, those in need, and believers receive the attention of the Lord and his followers. In this portrayal, Mark strongly suggests an open and expansive view in regard to others. In fact, he challenges those who serve to offer quality love and care to all regardless of their cultural and religious background or response. Professional ministers today find themselves working with a variety of people in expanding religious and cultural spheres.

Since the responses to the ministry of Jesus vary in the Markan narrative, success does not appear to be a criterion for effectiveness. In fact, Jesus receives outright rejection as well as misunderstanding. It might be good for the ministers of today to reevaluate ministerial effectiveness, and to assess their personal responses to acceptance and rejection. This is particularly important in a period of transition, as we have observed.

While certain disciples almost become "professional" ministers in Mark's gospel, the writer urges against an exclusively professional attitude. Likewise today, the servant qualities are again being emphasized for all baptized Christians, and for professional ministers.

Mark also demonstrates the necessity of various rhythms in the ministry of Jesus and the disciples. The committed Christian today must likewise insure time for leisure, retreat, prayer, and personal development, as well as for active involvement. Religious from their experience, can help laity to avoid burnout, and both can concentrate on balance. Balance and integration are the strong underpinnings of effective ministry and an authentic spirituality. Growth in faith is always a priority for the Christian minister, and it is enhanced by educational development and quality leisure.

The witness of living and working together is another value presented in Mark's gospel. In today's church, Mark challenges religious, laity, and priests to be signs of unity and love to believers and to the world. In fact, Mark urges all persons to broaden their views on ministry and ministers, and to collaborate for the sake of the gospel.

In the gospel of Mark, the writer presents the person of Jesus, discipleship, and ministry as interrelated themes. Together these three perspectives reveal the fuller meaning of Mark's proclamation, and offer new challenges for the contemporary believer. While we have focused on the aspect of ministry in the early church, it is clear that the gospel can speak to ministry in any period. In terms of our own considerations regarding our effective involvement in ministry, the gospel reinforces priorities in life as well as in ministry, rhythms for leisure and service, special moments and key experiences for those with a special commitment to ministry, and a communal concern that we are a sign and a support to one another. Ministry is an expression of our Christian identity and, in many ways, Mark challenges us to savor the various aspects of ministry, to continually expand our horizons, and to take as part of our commitment to ministry, an encouragement and fostering of ministry in others. These scriptural insights reinforce the approaches in this book.

CHAPTER 6

PAUL: Effective Ministry As A Leader In The Early Church

For many persons involved in ministry today, their ministry is a ministry of leadership or implies the exercise of leadership in certain situations or with particular groups. Scripture not only contains some powerful statements on leadership, such as Jesus' challenge to his disciples not to lord it over others like the pagans, but it also presents us with religious leaders in action. An outstanding example of a leader in the early church is the apostle Paul. We see him in action in his letters to various communities, which offer a unique perspective on this person, the leader, and his ministry in the early church. Again, as in our examination of Mark's gospel, scripture offers us insight, direction, and principles, which speak to professional ministers, pursuing personal fulfillment and effectiveness in their service of others. Perhaps, in understanding Paul, we will also see the parallel and the perspectives for Christian leadership today.[1] This examination of the letters will offer us a model for our ministry, and provide some cautions as well.

Any assessment of Paul as a leader must take into account several prime factors. As a person, Paul encompasses both greatness and limitations, gifts and liabilities. His personal qualities are strong and dynamic, making him the focal point in the early Christian churches. Vision and commitment are evident in his words and responses. Indeed, Paul is a religious leader who identifies his unique call and conversion as the turning point in his life (Gal 1:11f). He understands his apostolic mission in terms of this experience, and preaches the gospel because of the Lord's revelation to him (Rm 1:5-6). Furthermore, Paul's authority is established consistently as from the Lord, an authority to be exercised as a servant of others.

Paul responds to the unique situation of the various churches, and addresses the issues of importance. He is likewise able to deal with diversity with varying degrees of success, utilizing a spectrum of leadership styles. A *versatility* and *resiliency* characterize the person of Paul when he interacts with others in his letters. However, it is the presence of the Spirit of the Lord that ultimately directs and dominates Paul's perspective on Christian life and ministry. Guided by religious goals and principles, he perceives the situations and issues in the various churches as vehicles for growth for himself and others. Therefore, in order to understand Paul as a leader, we will take into account his personal attributes, his religious convictions, his exercise of authority, and his unique situational responses.

This chapter focuses on Paul as a religious leader, interacting with a number of communities in a period of transition and crisis in the early church. Paul's effectiveness is remarkable considering that he often deals with difficult and stressful situations. However, he appears to possess a resiliency that is important to all professional ministers. In our survey of the following letters, 1 Thessalonians,

Galatians, 1 and 2 Corinthians, Romans, and Philippians, the perspective of Paul will reinforce some contemporary approaches to leadership, effectiveness in ministry and a sense of personal satisfaction or fulfillment. Both scripture and Paul seem to withstand the test of time.

Early Leadership In Paul: 1 Thessalonians

In this first writing, Paul presents a Christian *vision* of life to his fledgling community. The church at Thessalonica is constituted as church because it is "... in God the Father and the Lord Jesus Christ" (1:1). This reality of God's continual activity is consistently presented by Paul to his converts, and it is this activity of the Lord himself that is responsible for the Christian growth of the community (3:12). Paul perceives believers as different, in essence and in practice, from their pagan neighbors; they are "... sons of light and sons of the day" (5:5). Paul's vision always revolves around this central core of Christian existence, namely, God's presence to, and God's activity in, the community of faith.

This openness to God is the essence of religious leadership and some implications certainly follow. If God is ultimately responsible for Christian life and growth (5:23-24), then Paul can rightly speak of Christians as always living in hope (4:15-17). Christian people, and the Christian community, can rely on more than their own human potential because God is at work in them. This realization itself offers hope. Furthermore, Christians are able to give thanks in *all* circumstances (5:18), because their perspective and their values are different. A Christian vision of life transforms the ordinary experiences of life, creates new attitudes, and challenges old values. The professional minister can reflect on these ideas with great personal benefit.

Because of his vision, Paul challenges the community to aspire to greatness in their daily life (4:11). A good leadership principle underlies the great visionary challenges of Paul, for he understands well that small plans or small ideas have little power to move people. *Creative ideas* and *vision* have the power to unite and to move others, even more than the presence of a charismatic person. But the vision must receive a positive response. In Thessalonica the new community is still in the initial enthusiasm of its recent conversion, and so Paul's words resonate with them. Creativity and vision are important for the professional minister today. But, as in the early church, the vision must be supported by the community.

Paul's perception of the essence of Christian life is intimately connected to his understanding of *authority*. The apostle does, in reality, exercise some kind of authority in the churches. Rather than by coercion or imposition, Paul generally persuades the Christians by his word and example. He is convinced that what he desires for them is a requirement of the gospel. He consistently bases his authority and the legitimacy of his teaching in God and on the word of God (1:5; 2:13).

The gospel/word which the community has received is powerful (1:5a). For Paul, it is this powerful word of the Lord that verifies his instructions and his theological reflections (4:2, 15-17). Paul also aligns himself with the prophetic tradition of the Hebrew Bible. He understands his authority and his role as a missionary in terms of his possession of the word of God. However, Paul still asserts that leaders should earn the respect of their followers because of their ministry (5:13). Position or status as a source of esteem, and consequently as a source of authority, is unheard of in Paul. In this letter, Paul shares and delegates the authority he has received from the Lord. A vivid example is Timothy who is not only sent to Thessalonica but is given the responsibility to assist the community as Paul himself would have done (2:17ff). These approaches reflect our current directions in ministry.

Because of his *reliance on personal relationships* with individuals and with communities, Paul's leadership becomes situationally and existentially developed. The apostle's emphasis on relationships is a creative element in his own exercise of leadership and goes beyond the Hebrew prophetic tradition. The prophets emphasized universal issues, such as injustice, with little attention to individual situations of injustice within the community. Paul finds the people, as well as the situations, an essential part of his work. Indeed the apostle's utilization of others is outstanding in the period of the first century. He enlists full and part-time helpers on his missionary journeys, and has quite a substantial company of co-workers. In his approach to missionary work, Paul frequently distributes the responsibilities for leadership among his colleagues. Considering Paul's strong sense of himself, this is quite remarkable.

Paul's relationship with the Thessalonians is very good and he utilizes his relationship with the community to challenge the Thessalonians to continue to assume responsibility for one another. He reminds them of his work among them (2:9), and exhorts them to apply all they learned from him to their own lives (4:1). In a concrete manner, Paul describes their roles, and in so doing he places the responsibility for community growth and development within the group itself (4:18; 5:14). Ministers are models for others, but ministers also awaken others to their own responsibility, as we have observed in chapter 3.

Paul's fostering and urging of communal responsibility is intimately connected to his vision of Christian life. In this letter, a positive relationship with the community is translated into a positive challenge for their continued growth and development. Paul also seems to have the ability to take concerns and to change them into realistic challenges. Furthermore, these teachings and admonitions are usually presented in a positive fashion (5:14-21), rather than emphasizing the negative side. As a leader, he *affirms* the good in the gospel and then *exhorts* them to continue making progress (4:9-10).

Not only is Paul confident in this letter, but the Thessalonians turn to him for direction. While he does not appear to be an unusually gifted person in this early phase of his ministry, Paul's perception of himself and his apostolic role, is closely associated with the vision of God's activity in him and in others.

Paul's *early leadership* as seen in 1 Thessalonians, is indicative of what is fully developed in the later letters. Paul is personally involved with the community, and his life is intimately bound together with the life of this church. Paul is creative in his exercise of leadership. In writing this letter, he builds on his earlier proclamation of the gospel. He utilizes *thanksgiving* to an extraordinary degree with this community (1:2-10; 2:13; 3:9-10), affirming them in their Christian lives. Paul clarifies, offers insights, and gives directives to the church (5:27). He discerns his leadership role as *directing* the early missionary endeavors, while always being at the service of others. Paul begins a new aspect of his ministry in writing to the Thessalonians, and he is already a leader with great potential.

Dealing With Crisis: Galatians

The letter to the Galatians affords us the opportunity to assess Paul's leadership ability in a crisis situation. If the letter to the Galatians is animated and argumentative, the writer is no less so. Paul is an intensely human *person* who feels deeply. In his range of emotions, from astonishment and disappointment, to the tender image of a mother giving birth, he radiates a personal sensitivity. If a leader's openness to emotion significantly expands his or her understanding of people, then Paul should understand others well. Paul admits to perplexity (4:20), is often ironic in his statements (1:6-7), sarcastic in his response (3:1), and blunt in his assessment (2:14; 5:12, 17). There is an urgency in his tone, and his letter overcomes distance and lack of physical presence. The personal qualities of Paul seem to be decisive. *In ministry today, people look for personal qualities, not simply quality service.*

The literary genre utilized by Paul suggests a carefully written piece with skillfully interwoven arguments. The arguments are strong and varied and they encompass the entire correspondence. The form of apologetic speech indicates a dialogic component in the development of the narrative. Paul responds to a situation and to issues raised by opponents of his gospel. In his response, Paul conveys an ability to be selective on the level of issues [there is one central one], and a skill in by-passing many details while focusing on principles. Paul has a certain *ability to identify problems* and a *decisiveness* which seems to be enhanced by his strong personality.

As a preacher, he is accustomed to persuasion and to pleading as well as to revealing his zeal and religious commitment. The homogeneous Galatian group is open to persuasion, and Paul is *confident* in his ability. Furthermore, Paul passes a kind judgment on the community, saying that something irrational and untoward must have happened (3:1; 5:7). Yet he warns (5:21), exhorts and rebukes them (5:1f) because a vision of Christian life is at stake. How interesting for us as professional ministers. We are expected to be strong leaders and dedicated Christians, to set priorities, be sensitive to others, and at the same time our people want us to be a prophetic voice and to challenge when indicated. There is a similarity between Paul's situation and ours.

Paul's *establishment and utilization of his authority* as an apostle strengthens his position as a religious leader. Paul's authority as a servant of Jesus Christ is divinely revealed. His theological insights are also inspired by God (1:11-16). Paul refutes anyone who will challenge his integrity or his gospel.

It is a religious experience and a revelation which give Paul his *insight* and *ability to assess* the situation in Galatia. In responding to the situation in Galatia, Paul not only skillfully identifies the main issue as the Jewish/Gentile question, but develops his argument and theology to address the problem appropriately. If something irrational has happened, Paul uses a rational approach to counter it. If the group has been swayed, Paul confidently uses persuasion to convince them. Paul exercises his leadership by speaking directly to the community, by establishing his relationship with Peter and Jerusalem, and by undermining the theology of the opponents. The unity of issue leads to a unity of theme in this letter. Paul passionately confronts the problems with their ramifications. In fact, he acts as if he is at his wits' end (3:4) because his apostleship and his ministry are at stake.

The good situational leader applies principles creatively, rather than legalistically. Paul certainly advocates life without the law, provides few specific answers, and reflects deeply on the implications of believing in Jesus. Religious convictions are operative here. Because of this focus, Paul can proclaim unpopular ideas, such as humanness, weakness, and crucifixion (3:13; 4:4-5), which are transformed by Christian love.

It is said that Galatians breathes *conflict* and that no

other Pauline epistle is so dominated by *controversy.* Yet Galatians is also a very personal letter of Paul, in which we observe the ability of this leader in the midst of controversy and conflict. The opponents are powerful and clever, but so are the leaders in the early church.

Paul's initial response to the crisis is confrontation and anger. Galatians is the only letter in which Paul eliminates the usual thanksgiving and immediately moves to the heart of the problem, attempting to reconcile conflicting interpretations. However, it is an angry, brusque and pragmatic Paul who emerges in this letter, as he battles an identifiable enemy. Paul carefully suppresses the names of the opponents while drawing out the implications of their position (1:7-9). The confronting and defensive attitude of Paul betrays a possible personal disturbance. Paul is obviously dealing with powerful opposition and a turning away from his gospel by a sizable portion of the community (1:6; 3:1). This propels him into action that is both *spontaneous* and urgent. Paul deals with conflict and controversy with directness and strength, confidence and conviction. We perceive a passionate involvement with the issues, and little respect for persons and for traditions. Paul does not shrink from controversy, and he himself may even be an integral part of it because of his overpowering attitudes. In the letter to the Galatians, Paul earns both a positive and a negative assessment of his *leadership style*, a consoling fact for professional ministers in the contemporary church.

Many *positive* attributes can be noted in Paul as a *leader.* When his authority and his interpretations of the gospel are threatened, he responds with force, conviction and clout. There is no repression of anxiety, but instead a strong response theologically and ethically. Paul's arguments are based on tradition, factual knowledge, interpretation and experience. A certain degree of empathy and understanding is present. These qualities contribute to good leadership. Paul's approach is directive as he carefully presents his theological arguments. He anticipates a positive response by the community, because he also invites the community to enter into the arguments, and to draw some conclusions themselves. His insight into Christian life forces Paul to be hopeful (5:1f), and even radical (3:1), in his exhortations and theology. Crisis leads Paul to utilize his influence, persuasive ability, and argumentative spirit in order to clarify the issues for others.

However, if strength is an asset, there is also a *negative* side to a zealous exercise of *leadership*. Paul's vehement and articulate manner can confront a crisis situation, but can also threaten people. His rugged independence, identified as the most salient feature of his character, can be a blind spot for any leader. The question is raised: does Paul get beyond the personal ramifications of the issue in the Antioch incident (2:11f), and in the conflicting Galatian situation? Does Paul overreact to the inconsistency of Peter, and the betrayal of Barnabas and the community? Is Paul flexible and accommodating, or is he inconsistent? Does he respond appropriately or react negatively? The questions are important since consistent appropriate actions are constitutive of effective long-term results. In ministry today, it is still essential to ask questions and to evaluate effectiveness. We have seen in earlier chapters that this does reduce stress in the long run and make life for the minister more satisfying and fulfilling.

Paul may remain a paradox of humility and arrogance as he deals with issues, ideas and people in Galatia. However, the letter identifies the dangers of legalism and the distinctiveness of Christianity. Whether or not Paul is sensitive or dictatorial in his approach is still open to discussion. However, Paul's leadership in Galatia is probably the initial step in clarifying the distinction between Christian and Jew in a time of transition. His confrontational skills lead to dramatic results which can be described as alienating or integrating, depending on the perspective. He continues to offer insights to us in this transitional period of the post Vatican II church.

Dealing With Diversity: 1-2 Corinthians

In 1 and 2 Corinthians there is a broad continuity and a discernible change in Paul's leadership style. These letters are good examples of an early Christian leader at work. As the situation changes, new demands are made on the apostle. As the community reacts to his instruction, another approach is necessary. Professional ministers today recognize this dynamic between leader and follower. It can be a source of stress, or challenge, for the leader in ministry.

In 1 Corinthians, we see Paul exercising a *situational-leadership* approach as he responds to reports and to questions concerning life in the community. Since the oral reports and written inquiries are clearly distinguishable in this correspondence, Paul's rejoinders can be compared. It appears that the apostle is more aroused, angry, and condemnatory as he deals with the oral reports from Chloe's people (1:11f; 5:1f). He does not discuss the issues but speaks decisively, with little appeal to an authority other than his own. On the contrary, when he specifically mentions the Corinthians' letter, Paul's manner is calmer and more analytical (7:1f).

Paul establishes his authority as apostle and founder of the community and is never apologetic for his changes in opinion. He believes in the Christian's ability to discern, as much as he believes in his own legitimate exercise of authority. Therefore, there are no simple solutions to the problems as Paul consistently develops his earlier teaching. The religious leader, Paul, is capable of change as well as conviction.

Furthermore, Paul's ability to correctly assess the situation is enhanced by his ability to listen and to be perceived as a servant of the community (4:1). He reminds the Corinthians that his attitudes reflect his theological convictions concerning Christ and the church (2:1f). He calls for imitation of himself, because he operates from an authentic vision of Christian life (11:1). Likewise, he demonstrates his sincerity as he attempts to orient the Corinthian church to the realities of that life, which include suffering and weakness (4:11f). Paul is confident in his mission, an asset in good leadership. A self-confident, persuasive leader is very likely to facilitate group growth and change. While many demands are made on Paul, his thinking is clear and his directives well founded. He creates alternatives for the Corinthians as he pastorally attends to the issues presented by the group. He is skilled in modifying their weaknesses by building a theoretical framework for his assessments. The issues on food to idols and spiritual gifts are noteworthy examples of this approach (8:1-13; 12:1-30). Paul motivates the group, attempting to understand their positions, and consistently points to a better way of living their Christian faith.

Paul directs a great deal of his leadership effort towards *dealing with diversity*. There is a diversity of approaches, of roles, and of lifestyle in this letter. Paul prioritizes gifts and responsibilities within the community in direct opposition to the Corinthians' assessment of their importance (1:20-31; 12:8-10; 14:13-19). Genuine diversity and social stratification are not a problem for Paul who seems able to cope with these paradoxical demands. We see Paul's skill in this area as he attempts to achieve an integrating pattern of relationships within the community. Furthermore, Paul emphasizes corporate responsibility and cautiously encourages the development of local leadership (14:12; 26f). It would seem that as a leader, Paul addresses the complex issue of diversity by offering direction and insightful comments to the congregation. On the other hand, Paul himself is sometimes intolerant of opinions other than his own, as these letters also demonstrate.

An identifiable *strategy* seems to mark Paul's dealings with the Corinthian Christians. He is keen on establishing principles for operation, principles that preserve the integrity of Christian life and freedom within the community of faith. Once the principles are established, he applies them to the situations under discussion (7:14-24; 8:4-13).

The leadership of Paul is also evident in his ability to establish priorities. He sets priorities for his own ministerial involvement in doing what others cannot do. Whether it be preaching, instructing, or defining the parameters for decision-making and action, Paul's norm is always the gospel and the building up of the church. In addition, Paul utilizes persuasion, modeling, argument, and judgment to elicit personal and responsible decisions in the church.

Finally, Paul's strategy is seen in his utilization of the people with means in Corinth. Their enthusiasm, drive and commitment are necessary to initiate the fledgling community. Paul appeals to persons of his own social class and background, as a profile of his colleagues seems to indicate. However, he realizes the dangers of too close an identification and so addresses the majority of the community in his letter, not the select few (1:26-29). He also recommends that those in the upper echelon accommodate their behavior to those in the lower classes (11:33-34). In every age, a strategy for ministry leads to increased effectiveness.

Paul's *success* in 1 Corinthians is due in part to the religious justification of his life (2:1-4). He thoroughly appreciates his own personal gifts and his apostolic vocation.

He has the strength of character and the resiliency to contend with criticism and misunderstanding. Vigor and daring characterize the apostle at this stage of his ministry.

Paul is reasonably accepted by the community since they actively seek his advice. He is fairly successful in his endeavors since many of the issues in 1 Corinthians are absent in his later letters. However, Paul's success is tempered by the fact that the relationship between him and this church actually deteriorates in the intervening period.

If there is a veiled hostility in 1 Corinthians, there is outright opposition to Paul in 2 Corinthians. Any assessment of his leadership must take into consideration the fact that he is now *under attack*, not merely misunderstood. The situation of being opposed by intruders and by the community constitutes a crisis for Paul. Paul's authority is being questioned by those who view apostleship differently. It would appear that Paul understands the seriousness of the charges addressed to him personally, and as an apostle. He therefore attempts to maintain his position and the integrity of his mission (2 Cor 11:1-13).

While Paul's conception of his role is in sharp contrast to that of the opponents, he does not hide behind a facade or mystique of authority, but rather willingly and openly defends himself (11:5). However, the pressure of opposing styles of leadership and a contrary gospel seems to evoke a defensiveness in Paul's response. He appears to be deeply affected by this outright challenge, and so expands his theology of the cross, and even takes to boasting (11:21-33). While the content of his defense may be theologically accurate, it is the defensive tone that colors the argument. Paul, as so many professional ministers today, feels the pressures involved in the continual service of others.

Although he is no stranger to *conflict and diversity*, Paul now must deal with it in a personal manner. In some instances, however, Paul seems negligent in taking adequate precautions against misunderstanding (2 Cor 6:14; 7:1). He seems unable to perceive these difficulties as an essential component in group growth. Paul's ability to empathize and to accept others is not always demonstrated in 2 Corinthians. Rather, there is anxiety and distress in his all *too personal response*. The incompatibility of his ideas with those of the community calls forth a reaction rather than a response. Indeed, Paul's warmth and tenderness are not consistently evident. More apparent is his plea for acceptance, understanding and approval. It appears that Paul places too much importance on his work and its effectiveness, so that it hampers his ability to deal objectively with the issues. It is also evident that Paul's personality is unable to cope with the severe personal attacks in this situation and so he frequently resorts to inappropriate behavior. This position is very tenuous for any Christian leader.

The Corinthian community is undergoing change and development. Paul is being challenged in his *ability to change* and to encourage a new level of growth for his followers. He certainly attempts to provide an atmosphere of freedom in his relation with the Corinthians. They are free to express their concerns and to explore other viewpoints. But perhaps Paul reads too much into the developmental crisis and questioning in Corinth, and is too concerned about their exploration of ideas and its consequences. As we have observed in earlier chapters, a healthy distancing might have been in order.

In the letters to the Corinthians, a twentieth century observer is able to assess leadership in process. Because several letters and visits are a part of the material for assessment, a development and a change can be identified. Many acknowledge Paul's difficult apostolic life, as well as the difficulties among this group of Christians. Admiration for his stamina, consistency and zeal is easily justified. Paul is always concerned with serving this very spirited community and endeavors to utilize his gifts on their behalf.

However Paul seems to be a controversial figure, both accepted and rejected, as he treads through the difficult developments in Corinth. There is little restraint on Paul's part as he responds, reacts and defends. Certainly, Paul knew the Corinthians' weaknesses and yet he is almost overcome by adversity. He finds himself needing and ready to apologize (2:1-10). Paul seeks feedback and affirmation from his converts (6:11-13). Paul spends so much time with this congregation, and yet history gives him mixed reviews. Some say the church in Corinth was left in disarray and rebellion by Paul, never to become an influential force in Christian life. Others see his efforts bearing fruit. Certainly Paul is a unique figure in the early Christian era, as these letters testify. His gifts are balanced by limitations. However, while Paul's ultimate success in Corinth is open to question, his approach can offer some insights for contemporary leaders who are plagued with some of the same attitudes and difficulties that Paul faced. The fact that he does deal with adversity, conflict and opposition recommends him and arouses admiration. If we assess Paul's effectiveness as a leader over the longer period, then the Corinthian correspondence adds to our understanding of his effectiveness.

A Mature Leadership: Romans

The letter to the Romans is unique in that Paul is not personally known to the community. It also represents a new level of theological insight. Paul's leadership is likewise

Paul: Effective Ministry As A Leader . . .   93

distinctive in his anticipation of events and in his mature and balanced response to issues of importance.

The letter to the Romans represents a new integration of experience and a qualitative refinement of ideas, calmly and carefully presented. Paul seems to have pondered the meaning of his own experiences and those of others. In this letter, he is more concerned about his mission to preach, rather than to preach successfully. As an apostle, Paul is an ambassador as well as an organizer and a planner. He is more peaceful in his role in Romans (5:1), and is adept at diagnosing the situation from a distance. In many ways, there will always be a difference between Paul and the churches, but once this difference in lifestyle and mission is recognized, the ministry of each can be effective. Perhaps, in Romans, leadership is more a process than a person, as Paul creatively reinterprets the Jewish tradition for the Roman community.

The apostle exhibits a vigor, persistence, venturesomeness and originality in addressing the situation of Jewish and Gentile relationship in this letter. Not only is Paul able to raise consciousness and to clarify issues for the Roman church, but he is also at an advantage in regard to his imminent visit to Jerusalem (15:26, 31). In concrete ways, Paul defines Christianity, its mission and its goals in order to preserve its integrity. Paul is also aware that he is likely to engender conflict and dissent in Jerusalem by his strong christological definition of justification and its implications regarding the law and circumcision (3:21-31). However, he anticipates this response and prepares for it. Furthermore, Paul draws upon his apostolic authority to validate his missionary endeavors and his theological perspective. The apostle and theologian achieves new heights in his letter to the Romans.

These new levels of insight strongly indicate a growing

maturity in Paul as a leader. It becomes apparent in the formulation of a more universal application of the gospel and an expanded theological development (1:16-17). Reinterpretation of the message of Jesus, not mere repetition, is characteristic of Paul. As a converted Jew, Paul struggles with the problem of how to proclaim God's new salvific acts without at least implicitly repudiating the old traditions. He focuses on the broad issues of humanity and of sin, not simply on Israel's call and rejection (1:18-3:20). He also speaks paradoxically and recognizes some issues as irreconcilable (Chs 7, 8).

Since Paul is in an active, but transitional phase, as he writes Romans, the letter becomes an indication of the apostle's adeptness to rethink, clarify and broaden his initial concepts. Paul seems to have the intellectual fortitude and integrity closely associated with eminent leadership in its mature phase. The fact that he writes Romans after difficulties and misunderstandings in Galatia and Corinth is testimony to his stamina and resiliency. Professional ministers can learn from his example and perspective.

Paul's approach in Romans has been described as *diplomacy* at work. The defensiveness of the earlier letters by a threatened leader gives way to a sure, steady presentation and argument. Paul skillfully involves the reader in the logic of his argument and questioning by the extensive use of diatribe. It is interesting to observe the level of the conversation in Romans 1-11. Obviously, Paul thinks highly of the capability of the community to deal with difficult issues and sophisticated teaching.

Significant *changes* can be noted in Paul's attitude and approach as he prepares to meet this community for the first time. He is able to change his tone and his demeanor. He uses appropriate leadership styles and adapts to the needs of his followers, important dimensions of effective *leadership*.

Paul also focuses on the servant dimensions of following Christ and its implications for any apostle (1:1; 15:8). Perhaps, more than any other aspect, the servant is characterized by listening, so that responses will be both appropriate and satisfying. Paul is attentive to the situation of Rome and of the broader church, and seeks to serve both the local and the larger community.

Evident, too, are his views of community and his concern about the *responsibility* of others. Cognizant of this fact, Paul emphasizes gifts and responsibilities as he exhorts the community in concrete and practical ways (12;4f). However, responsibility is presumed to be a mutual responsibility, designed to preserve group spirit and to build up the community. As a leader, Paul seems to elucidate principles and to apply them in given situations. He can be directive, but can also foster participation on various levels.

As a *facilitator*, Paul utilizes stimulating techniques to insure the involvement of the participants. The literary technique of diatribe teases the mind into active thought, and startles the imagination. Romans is filled with this rhetoric of questioning and answering, a contrived dialogue of sorts (2:3, 4, 6, 7, 9, 10, 11). The development of the lines of argument ultimately leads to a decision. Paul, as a successful leader, draws out, promotes and defends shared values. He builds on past experience in his historical appreciation of Adam, Moses, Abraham, sin, and the law. By drawing upon the past as preparation and as promise, he instills a renewed historical sense into his Gentile hearers, and fosters an expanding view of life for the Jews. Relationships are thus examined historically, and the community is caught up in the largesse of history. There is little room for threat as great vistas of engaging dialogue are portrayed. Paul also draws out the implications of his theology for Christian life as he skillfully and persistently describes the difference Christ makes (8:2f; chs 12-15).

In this letter the apostle exhibits an appropriate situational leadership style prior to his personal encounter with the Roman community (1:11). In many ways, distance seems to be to his advantage as he creatively, and maturely, refines his thought and his theological positions. Romans continues to challenge leaders to reflect again on the meaning and quality of their personal presence to any group. For Paul, great leadership development seems to be achieved in this period of transition and relative leisure, prior to his Roman visit and Jerusalem journey. Distance allows what presence does not. Paul is conditioned intellectually for the next stage in his missionary work, and the Romans are prepared for their personal encounter with the Apostle of the Gentiles. Paul's effectiveness in this context challenges the busy and pressured professional minister in the contemporary church.

Preparing For An Uncertain Future: Philippians

In his last public letter, the reader gains considerable insight into a formidable and effective early Christian leader. Paul's personal and pastoral character, as well as his extraordinary dedication, clearly emerge in his response to the Christian congregation in Philippi.

The leadership exercised by Paul in Philippians is correctly described as *religious leadership*. Paul's responses and assessments are motivated by strong religious convictions and goals (1:19f). There are no secondary distractions in this letter. Rather, life in Christ is the theological perspective that affects the exhortations to the community. Philippians is an important witness to Pauline spirituality (3:2f) in conveying the apostle's total identification with Christ, and with the mission of Christ. As an active spiritual leader, Paul challenges the Philippian church to cultivate this same mind and orientation in themselves (2:5). He also offers them models to emulate in himself and others (3:17). Paul, in Philippians, reminds us of the earlier discussion in Chapter 3 of the essence of spirituality for the Christian minister.

During a difficult imprisonment, Paul consistently expresses his total reliance on Christ and interprets the final outcome of Christian life according to this standard. In facing death, Paul ponders the deepest realities of his existence (3:7-16). He shares his longings, priorities and inner strength with the community (1:21).

As a religious leader, Paul places the interests and needs of the church above his own desires, incarnating the ideal of a servant style of leadership. He exercises his authority as an apostle and as founder of the church at Philippi by affirming (1:3-8), encouraging (2:1-2), exhorting (1:27f; 2:3-4) and confronting (4:2) the community. Because of his current experience, and his options, Paul seems to mellow on his dealings with opposition (1:18). He focuses his attention on the community and portrays communal life and attitudes in terms of unity, service and joy (2:5; 4:4).

Although there are theological reflections in the letter to the Philippians, a pastoral and situational response is the prime concern of Paul. The occasion of quarreling (4:2) is a good example of a leader's requirement to confront a delicate situation because of gospel values. Hampered by his imprisonment, Paul seeks alternatives in order to reinstate these influential women and diminish any negative vibrations within the group (4:3).

Paul delegates responsibility (2:19f) and prepares the group for his sustained absence (2:12). A spirit of detachment is appropriately expressed by Paul with regard to many circumstances of life (1:23; 4:12). This ability to distance himself seems to enable Paul not only to accept his fate, but also to offer more realistic solutions to problems. There is no defensiveness in Philippians, but rather, a steady reflection on the overriding goals of the gospel (1:18). With these values uppermost in his mind, Paul exercises a confident and a centered leadership.

The spirit and tone of Philippians reveals an *ability to change* on the part of Paul. Furthermore, Paul seems to simplify issues in this letter; there is little elaboration on the implications of opposition and diversity. With brevity, he presents his theological reflections and his spiritual insights (3:2f).

Finally, an unusual degree of *mutual acceptance* underlies the entire correspondence. The excellent relationship between Paul and the community enables him to strongly suggest options (1:19-26; 3:3-17) and to act appropriately (2:19f; 4:2f). Affirmation and love do not paralyze the apostle into ineffective behavior. Rather, these qualities enable both Paul and the community to deal with the harsh realities of existence (1:12f; 3:1f).

This letter to Paul's first European congregation, written towards the culmination of his ministry, crystallizes a personal and apostolic maturity. The apostle accepts the threat of death with equanimity and detachment. He likewise approaches his apostolic endeavors with similar attitudes (1:21-26). Because of the support of colleagues and friends, and a tested spirituality, Paul emerges as a religious leader par excellence. Paul enhances the caliber and quality of his leadership by gradually relinquishing his position. By thus insuring the future growth of the church, his attitudes and efforts deserve admiration and emulation by Christian leaders in ministry.

Paul's Leadership In Ministry

The letters of Paul reveal the positive and negative dimensions of the apostle's exercise of leadership. A Christian vision of life and of ultimate goals directs Paul's approach to the communities identified in the letters. His mission and ministry likewise evolve from a profound religious experience. However, while Paul is committed to his apostolic calling and endeavors, he is sometimes too attached to his success and loses perspective in his response, as indicated in 2 Corinthians.

Paul has an ability to work with a variety of groups. In Thessalonica and Philippi, a good personal relationship and a deep empathy enable him to affirm the community, challenge them on the level of growth, and accept suffering because of his theological convictions and beliefs. In Galatia and Corinth, conflict, opposition and controversy enable Paul to identify issues and to present clear, strong, theological foundations for his positions. At times he becomes too personally involved, but more consistently, crisis and opposition enable him to develop a confronting and elucidating leadership style. With the Roman community, Paul clarifies and addresses issues in theologically creative ways, even though he has no firsthand acquaintance with the congregation.

As a leader Paul concerns himself with the growth of the group, while maintaining his strong influence and persuasive appeal. He encourages participation, but also uses directive forms of leadership. In utilizing delegation, he maintains his leverage and input on the central issues. Paul tends to delegate and to share more freely when a good mutual relationship exists. He is hesitant with the problem churches in this regard.

Not only does Paul exercise his leadership in a variety of

situations, but he also relates to a broad spectrum of persons. With select colleagues he shares deeply, developing and honing their leadership skills. He seeks to serve, rather than to dominate, placing a high priority on personal affirmation and support.

Paul exercises theological leadership in all his letters, but notably in Romans, Galatians, and 1 Corinthians. He develops a unique leadership response as different situations, groups and issues challenge his ability as a minister of the gospel. The apostle also believes in the ability of the community to discern the truth in faith, and encourages them in this area.

Finally, Paul relies on a variety of resources, backgrounds, traditions, gifts, colleagues, and the Lord himself, in order to spread the gospel message. He is a creative, dynamic and enterprising leader who is ultimately forgiven his mistakes because of his sincerity and profound religious convictions.

Paul And The Professional Christian Minister

While we have already drawn some implications for the Christian minister in this chapter, we can make a few other comments relevant to the topic of effectiveness in ministry. Although there is no best leadership style, and no best strategy for change, the most effective leaders adapt and augment their responses according to environmental and situational demands. Likewise, there is no ideal leader or leadership approach. Rather, leadership is an interactional response between leaders and followers in various and unique situations. While this assessment is certainly true for Paul, his religious convictions consistently determine the parameters and the quality of his response. He has experienced the Lord and he has a Christian vision of life. In the contemporary church, effective leadership will also integrate acceptable leadership approaches with deeply held religious values. Leadership styles will be consistent with a personal, and a corporate, religious identity. Paul is a model and an exemplar in the sphere of religious leadership.

As an apostle, Paul exercises his leadership during a period of crisis and development in the early church. Not only is there opposition within the communities, but his ministry coincides with the gradual separation of Christians from their Jewish roots. Critical issues emerge and a radical reorientation affects persons, families and groups. New, fresh theological reflection results as Paul addresses the difficulties. In the contemporary situation, the church is in another critical stage in its development. Roles, ministries, essence and identity are being questioned. If the letters of Paul offer any insight, it is that crisis can lead to growth. However, Christian leadership and theological vision are key factors in facilitating the appropriate responses within the community of faith.

The followers whom Paul encounters significantly affect his leadership. The dynamic between leader and followers can be dramatic and forceful. Responsibilities are heavy on the part of both groups. In the contemporary church, individuals in leadership positions are subject to an extraordinary amount of criticism and confrontation. While Paul offers us insights into dealing with opposition, it must be noted that the most satisfying experiences, and the deepest spiritual insights, emerge in the communities where mutual esteem, respect, support and affirmation exist. This reality challenges leaders and followers today to create an atmosphere where all persons can offer their real gifts to the church.

Finally, Paul's leadership effectiveness is not positively

correlated with the amount of time he spends with individuals, or with communities. Corinth was his place of residence for a long period of time, and the recipient of four letters from the founder of the church. Yet, Corinthians does not achieve the theological depth of Romans, or the revealing spirituality of the letter to the Philippians. Perhaps this indicates that leisure and distance are essential ingredients for achieving a maturity and refinement in leadership and Christian vision. The "burned out" leaders of the church would do well to assess how they can best integrate experience and theology. With such an integrated leadership approach, a qualitatively different level of interaction and life will begin to emerge in the church.

Paul is a religious leader of unique caliber and quality. He is prophetic and charismatic, a servant and an apostle. For him, to live is Christ, and so the proclamation of the gospel, and the building up of the church, summon all his energy and commitment. Early in Paul's ministry, he exhorts a community in the sensitive and critical area of their responsibility towards their leaders. As Paul subsequently encounters a wide range of responses during his missionary activity, he must have poignantly recalled those words: "But we beseech you, brethren, to respect those who labor among you and over you in the Lord and admonish you, to esteem them very highly in love because of their work" (1 Th 5:12-13a). If we labor and grow in our ministry, as Paul did, then we, too, will earn the respect of others because of our witness and our service.

A rereading of the letters of Paul from the perspective of leadership opens us to a reinterpretation of the scripture for our situation and our times. In the apostle Paul we can identify the components of effective ministry, although the reality of success was not always his. Perhaps this aspect offers hope to us in our period of transition and crisis. We have a model in Paul as he deals with a variety of situations strikingly similar to our own.

Chapter 7

The Role Of The Leader In Promoting Fulfillment And Effectiveness In Ministry

Reflection on the ministry of Jesus and of Paul added to our discussion of ministry by offering biblical models to us. We have responsibility for ourselves as well as for those we serve. In order to grow in our effectiveness and to experience the fulness of life which Jesus promised, each professional minister would do well to understand his or her own goals and competencies, and to identify the rhythms in life and ministry that can lead to an integrated and fulfilling existence.

Throughout these pages, we have addressed the issues of burnout, stress, personal fulfillment, effectiveness and growth in ministry, and we have also identified a variety of creative approaches for those dedicated to the mission of the church. It is our conviction that the individuals involved in ministry are our greatest resources in the church. Because of this, persons in leadership roles have a special responsibility towards the women and men who work with them or under them. The pastor, personnel director, provincial, department chair, or program director have particular responsibilities for the growth of others. However, so do all professional ministers since they are leaders *and* followers depending on the situation, group, task, role or position. Everyone committed to ministry has an urgent responsibility to be concerned about effectiveness in ministry, the situations militating against it, and to explore new ways of enhancing human growth and personal fulfillment in everyone who exercises ministry within the community of faith. Having set this broad context for the discussion, we will now explore the role of the leader in the management of human resources and identify some concerns in this area.

The Role Of The Christian Leader

As has been noted, leadership in the church today is leadership exercised in a time of crisis within the believing community. An aspect of the crisis is the change in the roles of priests, religious and laity, and the consequent new expectations concerning these groups surfacing in all quarters of the church. The church is in a period of transition, and those involved in ministry are asked to serve in this difficult period of shifting responsibilities and developing understandings of ministry and ministers. Leaders, if they are effective, are individuals capable of dealing with crisis, transition, uncertainty, tension, and conflict. Not only is great resiliency required of leaders in the church today, but also great courage, because of an added responsibility to address delicate issues, to challenge oppressive tendencies and institutions, and to heal wounds. This ability or inability to assume such responsibility on the part of leadership profoundly affects the quality of ecclesial life and ministry. The Christian leader must have great facility in assessing situations, and in responding with appropriateness and timing.

This component of leadership will reduce stress and foster human development in professional ministers.

Most importantly however, we can describe the role of the leader within the church as one of *spiritual leadership*. In essence, spiritual, or Christian leadership fosters the growth of the community of faith by recognizing the competencies and abilities of the members, and by fostering responsibility for the use of these gifts among all the baptized. The Christian leader articulates gospel values in order to challenge the lived response of the community. Christian leadership implies, therefore, a grounding in faith, an understanding of scripture, a vital awareness of the essence, and role, of the church in the world. For the Christian leader, techniques and skills are inadequate unless these competencies are directed by other values.

Furthermore, the leader in ministry must embody significant Christian values in a visible and a viable manner. The leader is called upon to model what he or she articulates. In reality, the best contribution that can be made for long term effectiveness and burnout prevention is a new image of the Christian leader, and a new model of the professional Christian minister.

The role of the leader in the management of human resources in ministry emerges, then, from at least three realizations. First, the leader is keenly aware of the crisis within the church and its effect on dedicated Christians, especially church personnel. Secondly, the leader is aware that the exercise of leadership within the community of faith is properly identified as Christian leadership. Thirdly, the leader is aware that there is a need to model a new approach to Christian life and ministry. Having identified an overall perspective, we can now address the specific areas of concern.

Promoting Personal Fulfillment And Effectiveness In Ministry

If the leader within the church is to exert a positive influence on those involved in ministry and, thereby, insure the positive growth of persons in ministry, then several areas deserve attention. These issues can be discussed under the categories of personal growth and fulfillment, burnout, integration, the environment, evaluation, approach to change, and creativity. While not exhaustive, these areas of concern are inclusive, and offer a broad approach to the longevity of ministers in their work in the church.

Those who work with others in the various forms of ministry within the church must, first of all, actively commit themselves to the reduction of the stress that leads to burnout among church personnel. This active commitment to the *prevention of burnout* implies an identification of stressful situations as well as of the stress tolerance of the individual involved in a particular ministry. Many times this information can be obtained through conversation and discussion, but the utilization of coping scales, stress indicators and personality inventories should not be overlooked. Prevention of this contemporary dis-ease also includes a wholesome and healthy approach to life. Because of an overemphasis on work and productivity within church institutions in the past, it is often necessary to reeducate professional ministers in their middle years. Educational efforts can focus on nutrition, exercise, relaxation, relationships, theology, and spirituality, in order to correct a one-dimensional approach to life that is characteristic of so many highly dedicated people. Prevention also includes a periodic monitoring of progress, and the ongoing discussion of the various components of prevention among peers. While leaders must commit themselves to addressing this problem of burnout, the awareness and the collaboration of the persons involved in church ministry is essential. The prevention of distress or its reduction is a collaborative effort.

Related to the prevention of burnout is a positive concern for the growth and development of the whole person. Persons who are capable of using stress to their advantage, and who are fulfilled in their ministry, usually have proven ability to keep a good balance in their lives. The *integration* of life and ministry is a goal for church leaders and dedicated Christians. It is the ability of persons to bring balance to all aspects of their existence, and to easily move from one phase of life to another. Integration includes the integration of knowledge on the part of the professional minister, not only a knowledge of the job, but also an understanding of scripture, theology, ecclesiology, and themselves. This integration implies that knowledge leads to insight that will eventually result in new convictions lived out in ways consistent with Christian belief. Integration also extends to the family or community experience. Likewise, we thus consider friendships and peer relationships within the ministry team and their level of maturity and integration. If leaders are to foster wholistic development among professional ministers, then all aspects of an individual's life will be viewed in their relational dimensions. Often reactions in a meeting are the result of pressure exerted elsewhere, or of unresolved issues of a more personal nature. It is essential for the leader to foster a wholistic and integrated approach to life, in order to enhance his or her ministerial effectiveness.

The *environment* plays an important part in the performance of ministry. The work environment can usually be more conducive to a relaxed attitude. Often the utilization of appropriate color decor and arrangement makes a decided difference. The amount of money available or spent is not the prime issue. The utilization of the creativity of personnel to enhance their own environment can produce the desired result.

The atmosphere within the church as a whole is likewise a concern of the leader within the community of faith. Injustice, oppression, misunderstanding, static institutions, and legalism are some of the more obvious issues to be addressed. The leader can also identify positive positions and hopeful situations in order to turn the prevailing tide of doubt, cynicism and hopelessness among many in the ministry. At the same time, leaders are called upon to be keenly aware of the tensions in society, and the stressful conditions of living in the contemporary world. The sources of stress which predispose persons to burnout, or hamper effectiveness, are found on all levels of life in the church *and* in society. Awareness of negative elements often leads to action. Church leaders are encouraged to be involved with ecclesial and global issues, knowing that the environment affecting every person in ministry is broader than the pastoral team or the job at hand. The leader in ministry addresses the quality of work life from a very broad perspective.

The leader utilizes *evaluation* as another component in human resource management. On-the-job evaluation, carefully designed and effectively administered, is essential in giving persons a good understanding of their strengths and of suggested areas for improvement. Personnel evaluations by superiors, colleagues and those served can be enlightening and affirming for the person in ministry. Often counseling and various forms of assistance are subsequently offered to the individual who is unable to cope with stress. Programs can be developed to deal with potential problems. A good evaluation process can be utilized for a variety of purposes, and the Christian leader is urged to be fully aware of its potential.

Furthermore, leaders do well to develop an evaluative mode of thinking. For example, an understanding and assessment of motivations in ministry could be valuable in determining the satisfaction, and the energy, of church personnel. Ministry itself, as well as the professional minister, periodically needs to be reevaluated. Various forms of ministry are no longer necessary in the church because the needs are met by other groups or resources. Likewise, the Peter Principle can affect professional ministers, and so we suggest a reevaluation that includes skills, educational preparation and potential for career development in terms of the present ministry. The serious questioning of how placements are made, and a study of various placement options, can also insure the right individual in the appropriate ministry.

Because those involved in church ministry are living and working in a church in transition, leaders must be concerned with the whole phenomenon of *change*. As we have already seen, change is inevitable, but it is not always easy. While change occurs daily, it is not necessarily appropriate. It is essential for all persons ministering within the church to understand the process of change on a personal and institutional level. We can plan for changes by setting goals consistent with current theological reflection and situational needs. These goals must reflect the community's vision of church, and not simply result from attempts to better the present situations. Likewise, individuals must be able to identify reactions and responses resulting from transitions with their inbuilt tensions. Ministerial leaders should possess the skills needed for directing and advising church personnel who are in the midst of transitions, or who are anticipating major changes. The ability to dialogue, as well as to discuss, is an important quality for the leader in ministry. If professional ministers can share appropriately, and inclusively, with their colleagues, then the support needed in times of change will be developed in the sharing itself. Professional ministers who understand, accept and support one another will discover new approaches to change, and will themselves become a supportive intervocational group.

Finally, an area of concern for the Christian leader is *creativity*. Creativity testifies to resiliency, integration, fulfillment and growth, in ministry and in the minister. The aspects of creativity are the ability to dream, the possibility of a prophetic posture, the formulation of an ideal. For many dedicated persons in the church, these creative life orientations are merely a memory or an elusive dream. Christian leaders are in a position to be aware of the presence or the absence of this creative ability in their personnel. Christian leaders can foster its development. The components of a creative dimension in life and in ministry surface in periods of reflection, relaxation, significant personal encounters, and leisure. These qualitative moments are not experienced in a few fleeting attempts during a busy work day, or in superficial passing conversations. Rather, leaders can begin to exert their influence in order to change structures, and reeducate towards the pursuit of quality in their own personal lives. Dedicated people need periods of reflection, a retreat, a time for relaxed sharing together, a fun experience. There are visible benefits for the professional minister and for the ministry itself. Leaders, by their own approach to life, can encourage personnel to develop attitudes, and a lifestyle, that will insure the fostering of new creative energy. Furthermore, leaders can begin to assess the work situation itself, the parish, university, diocesan office, hospital, or school, in order to determine the changes that will insure the development of this Christian aspect of life.

In these select areas of concern, the role of the Christian leader begins to emerge. While responsibility for ministry and the management of human resources is shared within the church, the person exercising leadership in a given situation is often perceived as a model for the group. Perhaps a reflection on this dimension of a leader's role will enhance leadership within the church, and also insure the full development of professional ministers.

In these pages we have been keenly aware that as Christians dedicated to and involved in ministry, we carry "this treasure in earthen vessels" (2 Cor 4:7). Likewise we are conscious that "it is God who establishes us . . . in Christ, and has commissioned us; he has put his seal upon us and given us his Spirit in our hearts as a guarantee" (2 Cor 2:21-22). There is a fragility and a strength that we all possess. If we constantly recognize both of these realities, we can be real "ministers of God," effective and fulfilled.

Endnotes

CHAPTER 1

1 See Leonard Doohan, *The Lay Centered Church*, for a synthesis of the theologies of laity, an assessment of the contemporary church and perspectives on lay spirituality.
2 I am aware that the issue is broader than burnout as described in the literature. Mid-life crisis/transitions often elicit similar responses. Also, burnout in its last stages results in leaving the profession/ministry. Therefore, while establishing a context for personal fulfillment and ministerial effectiveness, I am also aware that the stress must be handled in the pre-burnout stages.

CHAPTER 2

1 See Helen Doohan, "Burnout," pp. 352-355, for a survey of recent literature and summary of aspects of the problem.

Because burnout is sometimes used as a catch-all phrase, there is a questioning as to whether the specific phenomenon actually exists. Responses to questions of clergy burnout range from no problem at all to a problem of epic proportions. The reality is somewhere in between. The actual extent of the syndrome among church personnel is our concern in this section.

In a seminar at the NACPA (National Association of Church Personnel Administrators) convention in Detroit in October, 1983, Joseph A. Fichter, S.J. presented the results of his study on the *Health, Work and Quality of Life of the American Catholic Priest*. Although the presenter announced that the clergy were in no danger of burnout because their health and life expectancy were far above average, the audience composed primarily of clergy strongly disagreed. The researcher conceded that one in sixteen clergy were potential burnout candidates and that the incidence was higher among parish priests who were 25 years ordained. However, according to his extensive study, there was no real problem to contend with or to address. Physical symptoms were his research variables in over 4,000 respondents.

The response of the clergy present, however, indicated a concern regarding colleagues in ministry. All present knew priests who could be described in typical burnout language. In addition, according to a U.S. Bishops' study, there is a hesitancy on the part of those 25 years in the priesthood to recommend that vocation to others (see Lauderdale, p. 152, where he speaks of burnout contagion. [It should be noted that a recent study (1983) indicates a change in the attitudes of priests toward their ministry]). Why? Certainly the symptoms of burnout, especially the overwhelming negative aspects, create a difficult portrait, making these persons poor role models.

What is causing the hesitancy and stress if others in the same situation are increasingly aware of burnout even if a particular person is not? The concern expressed by many of those involved in ministry is a legitimate one even if only a small number is affected. We are speaking about the diminution of service of the best people in a given profession and the personal happiness of those who are among the most caring of individuals. Furthermore, since the final stages of burnout are debilitating to the point of leaving a profession or ministry, the problem is best addressed in the pre-burnout stages of stress. In many ways, whatever we choose to call the problem, its early manifestations need to be identified.

Some available statistics can contribute insight into the dimensions of the problem. In summary charts on clergy and religious trends comparing 1965 and 1980, the numbers of active diocesan priests declined by 18%, religious women by 30% and religious brothers by 35% (see Kinsella, p. 5). Projected growth into the year 2000 among these groups is also sobering (p. 7). The number of religious theology students has declined by 54% in 15 years and the number of novices in religious communities by 89% (p. 6). These general trends continue into the middle and late '80s, even though in certain areas falsely optimistic numbers are being suggested. Meanwhile over 2,000 persons (some 30% of all Catholic theology students) are being prepared for *lay* ministry (p. 10), and 47% of all full-time directors and coordinators of religious education are lay persons, mostly women (p. 8).

Church personnel as previously known in the Catholic church are on the decline and a new type of church minister is on the rise. Role conflict is affecting all committed Christians, priests and religious in a special way. With new ministries emerging, new leadership is also anticipated and expected. Do the priests and religious have the resiliency to respond? Even the question is stressful.

The ministry phenomenon should also be examined in light of some earlier research on clergy. In a 1977 study by Eugene Kennedy, 57% of a representative random sample of American priests were considered underdeveloped (see Kennedy, p. 120). Underdeveloped was described as having an identity closely related to the *role* of being a priest rather than to themselves as persons, a vocational choice based on *status*, allowing the *expectations of others* to shape their lives, having few if any experiences of intimacy, a lack of understanding of the emotional life, and *repression* (pp. 125-126). Only 29% of the clergy studied were seen as developing or able to move into new human realms with a sense of purpose. While the situation has changed with time, the seeming lack of the necessary qualities to live in a transitional church continues to be thought-provoking (see Sammon, pp. 37-38).

The present church situation lends itself to personal doubt about the right choice in life and a radical questioning of the meaning of Christian life and ministry. Church authority's unwillingness to grant dispensations from the requirement of celibacy itself contributes to the frustration that often leads to burnout.

Endnotes 115

The crisis experienced by religious is one of significance and spirituality (see Chittister, p. 203). Ministry for the future will consist in smaller, less institutional religious communities, ministering in new ways on behalf of a new set of people (pp. 202-203). A lifestyle that will be supportive of such groups will be increasingly essential. Since no viable models yet exist, the future will be characterized by tension and stress. Personnel directors, in particular, will have the ongoing challenge of dealing with a pluralistic group in ministry, an older group in terms of religious and priests, and a group needing ongoing education in interpersonal as well as ministerial skills. However, it should also be noted that those in specialized Christian ministry have some additional resources from their religious traditions that can facilitate new growth and development (see Browning, p. 30).

2 Alfred Kramer, "Burnout — Contemporary Dilemma for Jesuit Activists," *Studies in the Spirituality of Jesuits*, January, 1978 in Gill, p. 21.
3 Jerry Edelwich and Archie Brodsky, *Burnout: Stages of Disillusionment in the Helping Professions*. NY: Human Science Press, 1980 in Gill, p. 21.
4 Gill, p. 22.
5 Epting, p. 47.
6 Humowiecki, p. 33.
7 Carlton and Brown, p. 10.
8 Swogger, p. 30.
9 Jones and Emmanuel, p. 11.
10 Gill, p. 23.
11 Christina Maslach, "Burned-Out," *Human Behavior*, September, 1976 in Gill, p. 11.
12 Clark, p. 23.
13 Gill, p. 24.
14 Swogger, p. 31.
15 Gill, p. 24.
16 Carlton and Brown, p. 10.
17 Gill, p. 26.
18 Gill, p. 23.
19 Redfield and Stone, p. 153.
20 Kendall, p. 280.
21 Cristantiello, p. 643.
22 Kennedy, pp. 14-15.
23 Kennedy, p. 8.
24 Johnson, p. 36.
25 H. Freudenberger, *The Staff Burnout Syndrome*, Washington, D.C.: The Drug Abuse Council, 1975 in Clark, p. 39.
26 Gill, p. 24.
27 Kennedy, p. 11.
28 Reeves, p. 21.
29 Doohan, "Leisure," p. 162.
30 Reeves, p. 129.
31 Humowiecki, p. 39; Carlton and Brown, p. 11.
32 Gill, p. 26.
33 Carlton and Brown, p. 11.

34 Jones and Emmanuel, pp. 10-11.
35 Johnson, p. 39.
36 Cameli, p. 101.
37 Maloney, p. 112.
38 Doohan, "Leisure," pp. 162-163.
39 Doohan, p. 165.
40 Reeves, p. 125.
41 Lauderdale, p. 28.
42 Pines, p. 35.
43 Pines, p. 61.
44 Lauderdale, p. 33, suggests high risk and low risk jobs, groups and religions and also offers burnout indicators which suggest personal and situational responses.
45 Lauderdale, p. 106.
46 Lauderdale, p. 114.
47 Freudenberger, p. 183.
48 Lauderdale, p. 151.
49 Howard, p. 20.
50 Schuler, pp. 63, 460; and Howard, p. 21, treat significant factors leading to dissatisfaction.
51 Helldorfer, p. 36.
52 Helldorfer, p. 31.
53 Pesci, p. 62.
54 Pesci, p. 65.
55 Sammon, p. 206f, describes five stages from burnout to apathy.
56 *Origins*, p. 667.
57 *Origins*, p. 663.
58 Helldorfer, p. 35.
59 Lauderdale, p. 115.
60 Kinsella, pp. 82-89.
61 Kinsella, pp. 49-56.
62 Schuler, p. 459.
63 Schuler, p. 286; also p. 229.
64 Schuler, p. 54.
65 Pines, p. 115.
66 Lauderdale, p. 113.
67 Sammon, p. 219.
68 Pines, p. 149.
69 Pines, p. 132.
70 Pines, p. 132.
71 Howard, p. 33.
72 Lauderdale, pp. 53-55, offers some interesting responses to stress and burnout and, on p. 125, identifies some steps for redesigning expectations.

CHAPTER 3

1 Cameli, p. 103.
2 Holmes, pp. 57-60.

Endnotes 117

3 Ernest Larkin, in a workshop for the CREDO Program at Gonzaga University, explored the implications of the contemplative way for ministry.
4 Freudenberger, p. 86, observes: "In times of deep faith, (hu)mankind is able to achieve the ultimate in denial by embracing the belief that this life is merely a prelude, that death is not an ending at all but the most desirable of beginnings."
5 Doohan, "Leisure," p. 165.
6 See George Aschenbrenner, *A God for a Dark Journey*, for an overview of apostolic spirituality since 1970.
7 Holmes, p. 102.
8 Holmes, p. 48.
9 Holmes, p. 242.
10 Coriden, p. 5.
11 O'Meara, p. 193.
12 O'Meara, p. 148.
13 See Leonard Doohan, *The Lay Centered Church*, Chapter 1, for a development since Vatican II.
14 Dulles, p. 132.
15 O'Meara, p. 170.
16 O'Meara, p. 71; also p. 89.
17 O'Meara, p. 135.
18 Bausch, p. 32.
19 Schillebeeckx, p. 18.
20 See Thomas F. O'Meara, p. 82, for a development of these various ministries.
21 Cooke, p. 37.
22 O'Meara, p. 87.
23 Dulles, p. 123.
24 O'Meara, p. 159.
25 O'Meara, p. 136.
26 O'Meara, p. 150.
27 Kennedy, p. 11.
28 Jaffe and Scott, p. 182.
29 Jaffe and Scott, p. 186, quote Mihaly Czikszentmihalyi, a psychologist, who identified this concept.
30 Lauderdale, p. 35.
31 Helldorfer, p. 36.
32 Pines, p. 150.
33 See John A. Sanford, pp. 5-15, who explores these special problems for the ministering person.
34 See John A. Sanford, pp. 106-115, for a treatment of these suggestions.

CHAPTER 4

1 Freudenberger, p. 104.
2 Pines, p. 10.
3 I am particularly indebted to the CREDO Program, 1983-1984, for their responses to questionnaires, and for their conversations on the topic of burnout. Their comments are incorporated into this chapter.

4 Kinsella, pp. 82-89.
5 Pines, p. 62f.
6 Schuler, p. 54.
7 Schuler, pp.84-85.
8 Rhodes, pp. 20-21.
9 Wilder and Plutchek, in Paine, p. 114.
10 See Susan R. Rhodes, p. 22, where the possibilities of this practice from Japan, are explored.
11 Schuler, p. 229.
12 Schuler, p. 286.
13 See Randall S. Schuler, p. 461, for a discussion of the effectiveness of these suggestions in regard to the previously unemployed.
14 Pines, p. 138.

CHAPTER 5

1 All biblical references throughout the text, are from the Revised Standard Version, RSV.

CHAPTER 6

1 For a complete examination and assessment of Paul's leadership, see my book, *Leadership in Paul*, 1984.

Bibliography

Aschenbrenner, George. *A God for a Dark Journey*. Denville, N.J.: Dimension Books, 1984.
Baily, J.T. "Stress and Stress Management." *Nursing Education*, 19 (1980), 3-63.
Bausch, William J. *Traditions Tensions Transitions in Ministry*. Mystic, CT.: Twenty-Third Publications, 1982.
Boy, A.V., and G.J. Pine. "Avoiding Counselor Burnout Through Role Renewal." *The Personnel and Guidance Journal*, 59 (1980), 161-163.
Browning, Don. "Pastoral Theology in a Pluralistic Age." *Pastoral Psychology* 29 (1980), 24-35.
Cameli, L.J. "Stress in Ministry: The Response in Spirituality." *Chicago Studies*, 18 (1979), 87-96.
Canary, J.F. "Stress in Ministry: The Experience of Changing an Assignment." *Chicago Studies*, 18 (1979), 87-96.
Capps, Donald. "Erikson's Life Cycle Theory and the Local Church." *Pastoral Psychology*, 27 (1979), 223-235.
Cardwell, Sue Webb, and Richard Hunt. "Persistence in Seminary and in Ministry." *Pastoral Psychology*, 28 (1979), 119-131.
Carlton, P.W., and G.R. Brown. "Stress Game: Administer Roulette." *Thrust*, 10 (1981), 10-12.
Chittister, Joan. "The Future of Religious Life." *New Catholic World*, 226 (1982), 200-203.

Clark, C.C. "Burnout Assessment and Intervention." *J. Nursing Administration*, 10 (1980), 39-43.

Cooke, Bernard. *Ministry to Word and Sacraments*. Philadelphia: Fortress Press, 1976.

Coriden, James A. "The Contours of Ministry in the Eighties." *Social Thoughts*. Washington, D.C.: National Conference of Catholic Charities, Fall (1980), 3-9.

Cristantiello, P. "The Value of Stress in Formation." *Review for Religious*, 39 (1980), 641-650.

Doohan, Helen. "Burnout: A Critical Issue for the 1980's." *Journal of Religion and Health*, 21 (1982), 352-358.

————. *Leadership in Paul*. Wilmington, Delaware: Michael Glazier, Inc., 1984.

Doohan, Leonard. "The Spiritual Value of Leisure." *Spirituality Today*, 31 (1981), 157-167.

————. *The Lay-Centered Church*. Minneapolis: Winston Press, 1984.

Dulles, Avery. "Imaging the Church for the 1980's." *Thought*, 56 (1981), 121-138.

Drucker, Peter F. "Managing for Business Effectiveness." *Harvard Business Review*, 41 (1963), 53-60.

Epting, S.P. "Coping with Stress Through Peer Support." *Topics in Clinical Nursing*, 2 (1981), 47-59.

Freudenberger, Herbert J., with Geraldine Richelson. *Burn Out. The High Cost of High Achievement*. Garden City, NY: Anchor Press, 1980.

Gill, J.J. "Burnout — A Growing Threat to Ministry." *Human Development*, 1 (1980), 21-27.

————. "Stress, Sexuality and Ministry." *Chicago Studies*, 18 (1979), 45-67.

Grossnickle, D.R. "Teacher Burnout: Will Talking About it Help?" *Clearing House*, 54 (1980), 17-18.

Helldorfer, Martin C. *The Work Traps: Solving the Riddle of Work and Leisure.* Whitinsville, MA: Affirmation Books, 1981.

Holmes, Urban T. *Ministry and Imagination.* New York: Seabury Press, 1981.

Howard, John, David Cunningham, and Peter Rechnitzer. *Rusting Out, Burning Out, Bowing Out. Stress and Survival on the Job.* Toronto: Financial Post/Gage Books, 1978.

Humowiecki, S.R. "A Physician's Reflections on the Stresses of Ministry". *Chicago Studies,* 18 (1979), 29-44.

Jaffe, Dennis T. and Cynthia D. Scott. *From Burnout to Balance.* New York: McGraw-Hill Book Co., 1984.

Johnson, J.W. "More About Stress and Some Management Techniques." *J. School Health,* 51 (1981), 36-42.

Jones, M.A., and J. Emmanuel. "The Stages and Recovery Steps of Teacher 'Burnout'." *The Education Digest,* 47 (1981), 9-11.

Kendall, P.C. "Anxiety: States, Traits, Situations." *J. Consulting and Clinical Psychology,* 46 (1978), 280-287.

Kennedy, Eugene C., et al. "Clinical Assessment of a Profession: Roman Catholic Clergymen." *Journal of Clinical Psychology,* 33 (1977), 120-128.

————. "Stress in Ministry — An Overview." *Chicago Studies,* 18 (1979), 5-16.

Kinsella, John. *In Service to Church Ministers.* Cincinnati, OH: A NACPA Publication, 1983.

Lauderdale, Michael. *Burnout Strategies for Personal and Organizational life. Speculations on Evolving Paradigms.* Austin: Learning Concepts, 1982.

Maloney, G.A. "Eastern Christian Hesychasm and Integration." *Chicago Studies,* 18 (1979), 111-130.

O'Meara, Thomas Franklin. *Theology of Ministry.* New York: Paulist Press, 1983.

Paine, W.S. *Job Stress and Burnout. Research Theory and Intervention Perspectives.* Beverly Hills: Sage Publications, 1982.

Pattison, E. Mansell. "Psychiatry and Religion Circa 1978. Analysis of a Decade, Part II." *Pastoral Psychology,* 27 (1978), 119-141.

Paul, William J., Jr., Keith B. Robertson, and Fredrick Herzberg. "Job Enrichment Pays Off." *Harvard Business Review,* 47 (1969), 61-78.

Pesci, Michael. "Stress Management: Separating Myth from Reality." *Personnel Administration,* 27 (1982), 57-67.

Pines, Ayala M., Elliot Aronson, with Ditsa Kafry. *Burnout from Tedium to Personal Growth.* New York: The Free Press, 1981.

Redfield, J., and A. Stone. "Individual Viewpoints of Stressful Life Events." *J. Consulting and Clinical Psychology,* 47 (1979), 147-154.

Reeves, Joy B. "The Leisure Problem and the Role of the Clergy." *Pastoral Psychology,* 29 (1980), 123-133.

Rhodes, Susan R., Michael Schuster, and Mildred Doering. "The Implications of an Aging Workforce." *Personnel Administration,* 26 (1981), 19-22.

Sammon, Sean D. *Growing Pains in Ministry.* Whitensville, MA: Affirmation Books, 1983.

Sanford, John A. *Ministry Burnout.* New York: Paulist Press, 1982.

Schillebeeckx, Edward. *Ministry. Leadership in the Community of Jesus Christ.* New York: Crossroad, 1981.

Schuler, Randall S. *Effective Personnel Management.* New York: West Publishing Company, 1983.

Straus, Nan, and Anthony Castino. "Human Resource Development: Promise or Platitude?" *Personnel Administration,* 26 (1981), 25-27.

Swogger, G. "Toward Understanding Stress: A Map of the Territory." *J. School Health*, 51 (1981), 29-33.

U.S. Bishops' Committee on Priestly Life. "The Priest and Stress." *Origins*, 11 (1982), 661-667.

Index

Acceptance, 68, 69, 75, 98
Affirmation, 6, 8, 55, 82, 101
Anger, 29
Anxiety, 50, 85, 91
Aristotle, 18
Attitude, 8, 20, 24, 43, 67, 73, 85, 94, 110
Authority, 21, 65, 78, 80, 84, 85, 87, 90, 93
Authoritarian management, 13

Brown, G.R., 13
Burnout, 6, 9, 15, 20, 23, 44, 49, 53, 76, 103, 105, 106, 108

Carlton, P.W., 13
Change, 6, 7, 15, 17, 19, 51, 53, 91, 98, 109
Charism, 21, 33, 34, 35, 102
Church personnel, 6, 23, 25, 49, 105, 106, 109
Clark, C.C., 13
Collaboration, 4, 5, 30, 34, 41, 42, 43, 47, 51, 58, 72, 73, 74, 76, 107
Commitment, 3, 23, 59, 63
Communication, 13, 53
Community, 3, 19, 23, 28, 29, 32, 34, 40, 51, 72, 73, 74, 79, 87, 107
Confidence, 8, 83
Conflict, 22, 42, 50, 53, 84, 85, 90, 93, 99
Confrontation, 67, 75, 101
Conversion, 78
Cook, B., 39

Coping, 11, 12, 14, 17, 21, 53, 56, 106
Counseling, 17, 57, 108
Creativity, 43, 80, 81, 93, 100
Crisis, 3, 5, 12, 21, 23, 41, 46, 51, 68, 82, 85, 86, 90, 91, 102, 104
  management, 6, 46, 51
Criticism, 8, 42

Decision-making, 20, 40, 42, 46, 89
Decisiveness, 83
Delegation, 6, 8, 13, 99
Demands, 15, 32, 71
Detachment, 9, 97
Dialogue, 5, 30, 43, 53, 58, 59, 83, 109
Discernment, 5, 33, 39, 40, 46, 60
Disciple, 32, 37, 62, 63, 64, 68, 71, 75, 77
Distress, 6, 20, 50, 54
Diversity, 42, 88, 89, 90

Ecclesiology, 4, 37, 39, 107
Education, 4, 6, 13, 24, 56, 76
Effectiveness, 5, 6, 8, 19, 22, 23, 27, 38, 43, 44, 46, 47, 49, 54, 57, 59, 61, 62, 68, 72, 73, 74, 75, 77, 78, 79, 86, 89, 91, 101, 103, 104m, 105, 108
Emmanuel, J., 11
Enthusiasm, 14
Environment, 8, 19, 21, 30, 56, 100, 106, 107, 108
Evaluation, 16, 17, 24, 53, 106, 108
Excellence, 47
Expectations, 9, 12, 18, 22, 50, 54, 55

MINISTRY TODAY

Faith, 22, 28, 29, 39, 41, 46, 47, 64, 68, 71, 79, 88, 105
Family, 37, 107
Fear, 14
Feedback, 20, 24, 25m, 53, 92
Flow state, 44
Freudenberger, H.J., 15
Friendship, 24, 28, 57
Frustration, 21, 23, 45, 58
Fulfillment, 8, 18, 26, 47, 49, 54, 61, 62, 77, 79, 103, 104, 110

Gill, J.J., 13, 15
Guilt, 6, 13, 15

Hope, 38, 72
Human resources, 51, 104, 105, 110
Humility, 29, 70, 86

Idealism, 12, 15, 18, 23
Imagination, 30
Integration, 17, 18, 29, 30, 49, 52, 59, 60, 76, 93, 102, 106, 107
Intimacy, 14, 30

Job descriptions, 5, 52
Job satisfaction, 20, 26, 52
Jones, M.A., 11

Kramer, A., 11

Laity, 4, 7, 20, 33, 39, 41, 59, 76
    priesthood of, 32
Larkin, E., 28
Leadership, 4, 32, 35, 38, 40, 41, 59, 77, 79, 80, 81, 84, 85, 86, 87, 90, 101, 111
    crisis, 4
    religious, 96, 97, 105
    roles, 8
    situational, 16, 78, 84, 87, 96, 97
    style, 4, 13, 41, 94, 100, 101
Leisure, 16, 18, 24, 29, 30, 45, 54, 55, 60, 76, 96, 110
Lifestyle, 23, 51, 72, 88, 110
Liturgy, 4, 25
Loneliness, 6, 13, 29

Ministry:
    forms of, 23, 36, 38, 58, 66
    New Testament, 31, 33
    facilitating, 46
    future, 43
    response to, 31
    team, 66
Motivation, 8, 109

Needs:
    personal, 8
    other, 13, 31, 37, 40, 41, 66, 67, 71
O'Meara, T.F., 32, 39

Peak performance, 44
Planning, 17, 24, 52, 54, 93
    human resource planning, 24, 25, 51
Potential, 34, 51, 82, 109
Poverty, 7, 29
Power, 29, 30, 42
Prayer, 9, 24, 28, 30, 41, 46, 55, 58, 72, 76
    contemplative, 18, 28, 29, 46
Priest, 4, 5, 6, 14, 20, 23, 25, 39, 59
Priorities, 71, 72, 88, 89
Proclamation, 36, 64, 65, 68, 76, 82

Relationships, 28, 37, 45, 57, 63, 68, 81, 88, 95, 99, 106
Relaxation, 16, 26, 106, 110
Religious, 4, 5, 6, 7, 8, 20, 23, 25, 39, 51, 59
Resiliency, 20, 42, 45, 78, 90, 110
Responsibility, 43, 45, 81, 95, 103, 104, 110
    personal, 17, 25, 50
    family, 7

Sabbatical, 56
Schuler, R.S., 53
Self-assessment, 16
Self-awareness, 21, 43
Self-esteem, 22, 25, 29, 44, 50, 80
Self-knowledge, 16, 17, 28, 29
Servant, 38, 39, 70, 75, 78, 88, 95, 97, 102
Society, 19, 20, 108

Spirituality, 5, 17, 27, 28, 37, 39,
    43, 46, 49, 54, 55, 61, 76, 96, 98
Stress, 3, 5, 6, 7, 8, 9, 14, 24, 25, 27,45,
    53, 54, 86, 103, 105, 106
Structures, 4, 16, 22, 23, 38, 51, 52,
    53, 59
Success, 25, 69, 78, 89
Support, 6, 24, 71
Support systems, 17, 19, 26, 46, 54,
    57, 59, 110
Swogger, G., 11

Transition, 22, 75, 109
    mid-life, 9

Vatican Council II, 3, 21, 37, 41, 50,
    87
Vision, 30, 40, 46, 79, 80, 82, 88, 99,
    101

Wealth, 19, 29
Wholeness, 17, 31, 44, 45, 55, 107
Women, 4, 33, 35, 41, 42, 57, 58, 73
    97
Work, 19, 20, 22, 24, 31, 44, 52, 53
    54, 55, 60, 108, 110
World, 3, 5, 12, 29, 53

www.ingramcontent.com/pod-product-compliance
Lightning Source LLC
Chambersburg PA
CBHW050830160426
43192CB00010B/1969